Youth Sport in Ireland

The Sporting, Leisure and Lifestyle Patterns of Irish Adolescents

Seán Connor

The Liffey Press

Published by
The Liffey Press Ltd
Ashbrook House, 10 Main Street
Raheny, Dublin 5, Ireland
www.theliffeypress.com

A catalogue record of this book is
available from the British Library.

ISBN 1-904148-29-8

AN CHOMHAIRLE SPÓIRT

*Published with financial assistance
from the Irish Sports Council*

Printed in the Republic of Ireland by Colour Books Ltd.

About the Author

Sean Connor, PhD, has been a lecturer on the sociology of sport in Waterford Institute of Technology since January 1995. He previously worked in the Burren Outdoor Education Centre for County Clare VEC and also worked as a PE teacher in St Paul's, Monasterevan. He is currently leading a major research project into volunteerism in Irish society, which is funded by the Royal Irish Academy. Sean would welcome readers' comments or suggestions at sconnor@wit.ie

all important to see what exactly Irish teenagers are currently doing. If sport is already part of their lifestyle repertoire, why is that the case? If it is not, what are the reasons for this and what sort of options are most likely to make sport part of their regular lifestyle? By attempting to piece together the various parts of the jigsaw which make up the adolescent lifestyle, one can attempt to map leisure activity into a form to ensure that it at least makes up one piece of that lifestyle.

PHYSICAL ACTIVITY AND ADOLESCENTS

Whilst the importance of physical activity for present and future health has been firmly established (Bouchard et al., 1990), there is growing concern that an alarming number of Western European children in today's society are adopting inactive lifestyles (Sleap and Warburton, 1992; Thirlaway and Benton, 1993). In Ireland, the Department of Health is particularly worried about the level of heart disease amongst Irish adults. The mortality rate from heart attacks in the Irish population is over twice the EU average. The Irish figure is 238 deaths per 100,000 people as against an EU mean of 98 per 100,000 (Department of Health, 1995). As many of the lifestyle habits which lead to increased risk of heart problems begin in adolescence, this is an age group which needs to be specifically targeted as part of a preventative approach to health management.

Whilst there appears to be widespread agreement on the need for physical activity amongst adolescents, there has been considerable debate about the form that this activity should take. There has recently been a move away from strict prescriptive-type activity guidelines.[2] Cale and Harris (1993) point out that the presentation of rigid exercise prescriptions to children may result in turning many of them away from exercise for life. However, an international body (the International Consensus Conference on Physical Activity) has examined this issue in detail and has suggested guidelines which have gained widespread acceptance. These guidelines will now be outlined.

---

[2] In prescriptive exercise programmes, the nature, intensity and duration of the activity would be prescribed.

Physical Activity Guidelines for Adolescents

There is a certain basic metabolic rate of physical activity which is required to maintain fitness and general health. However, the level of physical activity varies from person to person and over time (Armstrong and McManus, 1994b) and is often described under four headings:

• Duration

• Frequency

• Intensity

• Type of activity (Montoye et al., 1996, p. 3).

A broad definition of physical activity is given by Caspersen et al. (1995, p. 11) when they describe physical activity as "all bodily movement produced by skeletal muscles that results in energy expenditure". However, for the purposes of this study, physical activity will be used as an umbrella term pertaining to both the structured (e.g. organised youth sport, school PE) and unstructured (e.g. after-school play) movement experiences of adolescents. The International Consensus Conference on Physical Activity Guidelines for Adolescents was convened to establish appropriate physical activity guidelines for adolescents in 1992. They established two key guidelines:

> 1. All adolescents should be physically active daily or nearly every day, as part of play, games, sport, work, transportation, recreation, physical education or planned exercise in the context of family, school and community activities.
>
> 2. Adolescents should engage in three or more sessions per week of activities that last 20 minutes or more at a time and that require moderate to vigorous levels of exertion (Sallis and Patrick, 1994, pp. 307–8).

These guidelines are used as the benchmark for assessing physical activity levels amongst adolescents. They offer a useful working definition of a complex area which is applicable at a practical research level.

THE MICRO-SOCIAL INFLUENCES ON ADOLESCENT DEVELOPMENT

Adolescence is a period of profound biological, emotional, intellectual and social maturation unmatched by any other period in life, except infancy. In first world countries, adolescence seems to begin before puberty as preadolescents adopt the dress and mannerisms of teens. This phase of one's life appears to continue well beyond the teenage years as many young adults remain dependent upon their families as a result of continuing in the education system, unemployment or limited earnings. The transformation from childhood to adulthood is characterised by tremendous variability from individual to individual. The physical changes can be dramatic. Emotions can fluctuate between elation and depression. Intellectual capacity may deepen and adolescents may gradually become capable of higher order thinking and reasoning. The expectations of family members, teachers, friends and society sometimes lead to confusion about issues of independence, conformity and responsibility.

Notwithstanding the definitional problems associated with the concept of adolescence, the process of moving from childhood to adulthood is frequently divided into three general stages of adolescence: early (ten to thirteen years), middle (fourteen to sixteen years) and late (seventeen until adulthood). During these transformations, several major physical, emotional and mental developmental tasks have been documented. These are:

- Development of self-identity and a sense of social responsibility;

- Acceptance of body image;

- Determination of sexual identity and role;

- Development of a personal value system and ethics;

- Transition from dependence on family to independence;

- Development of mature personal relationships, including sexual relationships; and

- Identification of possible career goals and acquiring the skills necessary for greater economic independence (Petersen and Gardener, 1989).

The potential effects of these developments on adolescent leisure and lifestyle behaviour need to be explored. There is much to be learned in relation to adolescents and this knowledge can be used in promoting strategies which drive, and in reducing constraints which limit, sports participation by adolescents. Therefore, these issues will be addressed in detail in later chapters, when analysing interviews conducted with a cohort of adolescents. However, there is significant variability in how individuals develop. Some of the factors which influence the adolescent's development are internal to the adolescents themselves. In particular, physiological and emotional pressures are internal while other influencing factors which originate from family, teachers, peers, significant others and wider society are external to the adolescent. It is the interplay of these forces which generates the uniquely felt, yet broadly shared, experience of adolescence. The outcomes for sport, physical activity and lifestyle patterns are a prime concern of this book.

THE MACRO-SOCIAL INFLUENCES ON ADOLESCENT DEVELOPMENT

Irish Society

This book further sets out to explore the social, psychological, biological and developmental factors which contribute to differences in the sporting and physical activity behaviour of adolescents living in contemporary Ireland. Of particular interest is the examination of certain social factors that may influence young people's participation rates in physical activity. Specifically, it sets out to examine factors including the role of socio-economic status, the role of the education system, gender and family and how these variables may offer possible explanations for differing participation rates in physical activity by adolescents. It is helpful in the first instance to examine the current setting of which the adolescents are a part. Irish society is rapidly changing and the complexity of this change is reflected by Gibbons when he said: "Ireland is a first world country but with a third world memory" (1996, p. 3). This section will therefore outline some of the recent changes in Irish society.

The lifestyle of the average Irish person has changed dramatically in the past 30 years. From being a Catholic, conservative and rurally dominated society, Ireland has embraced Europe with an enthusiasm that is possibly not reflected in any other member state. Arguably, one of the single biggest catalysts in this change in the Irish psyche has been the Republic's entry into the European Community in 1973. This has been evidenced in referenda on European issues where, prior to the first Nice referendum, the pro-Europe voters have to date had comfortable majorities. This country is now in the throes of becoming a more liberal, pluralist and indeed wealthy state. Divorce became law in 1996, a fact which would have been incomprehensible only 20 years ago. Even in 1986, a similar referendum was rejected by a two-to-one margin. Similarly, the people of Ireland elected two consecutive women presidents and the social agenda on such areas as gay rights are now largely pursued from a European Union agenda rather than from the church pulpit which was often seen to be a feature of the *old* Ireland.

Adolescents growing up in Ireland today are experiencing a very different type of society than their parents would have experienced and their attitudes are likely to be determined from the mores of this current era. The Irish adolescent is also growing up in a wealthier Ireland than their parents would have experienced, despite the recent downturn. This is because many areas of Irish society experienced rapid growth and increasing wealth in the last decade. The services sector and tourism in particular boomed. The number of visitors more than doubled from the period 1991 to 1996 (Bord Fáilte, 1996). Moreover, Ireland received substantial funds from the European Regional Development Fund to bring the infrastructures in Ireland up to European norms. In brief, the country during the 1990s was on the back of an economic boom and financial returns to the exchequer rose dramatically. The average industrial wage continued to rise above inflation, so the lot of the average worker improved. Working conditions have improved through the introduction of a statutory maximum working week of 39 hours and a guaranteed minimum wage to all employees. With certain exceptions, such as emergency personnel, each citizen is now legally guaranteed the time for leisure activities. The specific effects on the sporting, leisure and lifestyle patterns of adolescents of living in a post-modern Ireland will be examined in later chapters.

What is perhaps unique to Ireland, in comparison to our neighbouring countries, is that the scale and rate of change in Irish society is unprecedented. Gemma Hussey neatly summarised the profundity of these changes as follows:

> Irish society has changed more in the two decades leading up to the 1990s than in the whole previous one hundred years, going back to the Great Famine of the mid-nineteenth century. An inward-looking, rural, deeply conservative, nearly 100 per cent Roman Catholic and impoverished country has become urbanised, industrialised and Europeanised. Its political and social institutions are challenged by the realities of today, and in many cases are proving unequal to the challenge (1995, p. 1).

The leisure and lifestyle patterns of Irish adults were influenced by the norms of their times. In particular, sports such as the traditional Gaelic games would often have been the only ones available to them as they grew up and so these dominated the sporting interests of a number of generations. This book examines modern Irish society and assesses how the current cohort of adolescents is similarly being influenced by the society in which they are now growing up. De Knop et al. (1996) assert that Western societies have moved from being "survival" to "enjoyment" societies. If this is the case, it would be expected significantly to affect the lifestyle and leisure values and practices of adolescents.

Education

One reflection on our Celtic past was that Ireland was regarded as an "Island of Saints and Scholars" (Darcy, 1985, p. 4). Similarly, since Ireland achieved post-colonial status, there was initially from the 1920s to the 1960s a slow but steady increase in participation in second-level education. However, since the introduction of free school transport in 1967, the Irish public has embraced education with passion. Figures from Coolahan (1985) and from the Department of Education and Science (DES) show that in 1966 fewer than 10,000 people finished second-level education. By 1979, this figure had almost quadrupled to 36,000 and the increase continued to 1997, when the figure was 66,000 (DES, 1997). Demographic changes account to some extent for this demand for education, but there are significant social issues and values which have also accounted for this growth. Irish adolescents have considerably greater access to education than their parents. In the White Paper on Education (DES, 1995), it is a stated aim that 90 per cent of school-goers would complete their senior cycle education. Thus finishing second level and going into third-level education is now the norm for most Irish adolescents.[3]

Sport in Ireland

As a result of increased demand, the availability of participative sports, both in terms of facilities and variety, has mushroomed in Ireland in recent years. One significant development in the 1970s was the opening of the National College of Physical Education in Limerick. This was the first time the training of male PE teachers[4] was conducted in a coherent, educationally informed physical education curriculum in Ireland and many schools got their first PE teacher at this time. In tandem with this development, there was (notionally at least), the introduction of a broader curriculum[5] of sports in schools. This was also facilitated by physical developments such as the building of state-

---

[3] Third level education is taken to mean, in this case, all post-second-level education which is available in Ireland. This includes universities, colleges of education, institutes of technology and post-leaving certificate courses.

[4] Sion Hill and Ling Colleges had been training female PE teachers for several years prior to the opening of the National College of Physical Education in Limerick in 1973.

[5] There is an official curriculum for PE but the subject is currently optional. What individual schools actually offer as part of their PE programme is often determined by localised factors such as the expertise of the teacher(s) and/or facilities available and the amount of time allocated to the subject by the school.

supported community schools, a number of which had swimming pools, whilst most other schools built were provided with varying levels of sports facilities.

Until well into the 1980s, the Gaelic Athletic Association and their main sports, Gaelic football and hurling, were unchallenged in terms of playing numbers and spectator support. However, the 1980s and 1990s saw an unprecedented boom in other sports such as soccer, basketball and golf. The increase in soccer is mainly attributed to the success of the Irish national team in both European and World Cup competitions. Often termed the *golden years of Irish soccer*, the period 1986 to 1996, under the stewardship of Jack Charlton, saw unprecedented success for the Irish Association Football team. Basketball is an example of another sport which has caught the imagination of Irish schoolgoers, particularly girls. The number of girls playing basketball has increased six-fold in less than ten years. In 1988, there were 10,000 participants. The figure had risen to over 60,000 in 1997 (Irish Basketball Association, 1999). Golf has benefited from the increased affluence in Ireland and facilities have also been built to cater for tourism markets. Figures released by the Golfing Union of Ireland in 1999 confirm these trends. Over the period 1990–1999, the number of full members in Irish clubs increased by 60 per cent from 139,000 to 220,000. In general, facilities, variety and expertise have all improved in recent years. The perception of the political importance of sport is also evidenced by the designation of sport as a full ministerial portfolio in June 1997.

Significant contributing factors to active leisure participation include education level, transport, money, facilities and expertise (Veal, 1994). It should clearly be the case then in Ireland that participation rates should be at an all-time high. However, there are a number of factors which have limited physical activity rates in Ireland. Increased car ownership has resulted in the majority of adolescents being dropped to schools. Ireland has in recent years been blitzed by revelations of childhood sexual abuse and it is no longer perceived to be safe for "comely maidens" to dance at the crossroads. The rustic descriptions of children playing and growing up in rural Ireland as described by Alice Taylor in *To School through the Fields* is now little more than a romantic ideal:

> In the summers, we swam in the river and caught minnows with jam pots . . . we were reared as free as birds, growing up in a world of simplicity untouched by outside influences. Our farm was our world and nature as an educator gave free rein to our imaginations, unconsciously we absorbed the natural order of things and observed the facts of life unfolding daily before our eyes. We were free to be children and to grow up at our own pace in a quiet place close to the earth (1990, p. 9).

Whilst Ireland is no longer perceived to be a safe haven to play sports (if indeed it ever really was), consequently there is now a decrease in the amount of unsupervised play by young people. At the same time, the Irish adolescent does appear to have access to a wider range of sports than was available to their parents' generation. Similarly the influence of traditional Irish games would appear to be waning. Up until 1971, when "the ban" was removed, anyone who wished to play GAA sports was not allowed to play certain other sports such as soccer and rugby. Unlike their parents, the modern Irish adolescent usually has the option to play whatever sports he or she wishes. However, there is a definite trend towards "cocooning" which has been documented by writers like De Knop (1996).[6] It would appear therefore that modern teenagers may have advantages in their range of available activities but, conversely, they may be more constricted as to where and with whom they can partake in these activities. They also have widespread access to the competing attraction of television, computer games and the Internet so there may be pull factors towards passive leisure which may constrain physical activity levels.

---

[6] Cocooning refers to the growth in home-based activities and is often associated with the widespread watching of television.

Urbanisation and Demographic Trends

The concept of Ireland as a rurally dominated country has changed remarkably, particularly with Dublin becoming increasingly recognised as a top modern European city. Ireland is following world-wide trends for industrialised countries and has become a more urbanised society. Table 1.1 illustrates how Ireland has changed consistently and dramatically this century. At the beginning of a new century, Ireland is heading for a reversal of the 1900 balance.

Social and demographic changes have significantly impacted on the Irish population. Ireland had an unemployment rate of 19 per cent or 342,000 in 1986. With the recent economic boom this figure dropped below 5 per cent in 1999 (CSO figures) which is the lowest figure for over 30 years.

In line with international trends, serious crime and drug abuse figures continue to rise. There also appears to be a significant change in the nature of family life. Twenty-seven per cent of children were born to single mothers in 1996. Fifteen per cent of married couples are now separated and the numbers are expected to multiply as divorce becomes a fact of Irish life.

Table 1.1: Population in Towns and Rural Areas, 1901–1996*

Population	1901	1926	1946	1966	1971	1981	1991	1996
Town Population ('000s)	911	959	1,161	1,419	1,556	1,915	2,013	2,106
Rural Population ('000s)	2,311	2,013	1,794	1,465	1,423	1,529	1,512	1,520
Total	3,222	2,972	2,955	2,884	2,979	3,444	3,525	3,626
In Towns	*28%*	*32%*	*39%*	*49%*	*52%*	*56%*	*57%*	*58%*
In Rural Areas	*72%*	*68%*	*61%*	*51%*	*48%*	*44%*	*43%*	*42%*

* Town population is defined as all those people living in towns with a population of 1,500 or more.

Source: Central Statistics Office figures, 1901–1996.

As well as the sweeping social changes which are occurring, there is also the impact of technology on adolescent lifestyles.

Modern youths are often bombarded with technology as they get on board the information superhighways. Table 1.2 below shows the significant increases in both the availability of computers and the increasing access to computers in the home. Television is also influential in teenagers' lives. This has both positive and negative effects. There is also the globalising effect of television — Irish teenagers are watching many of the same programmes as their American and British counterparts thanks to satellite television and videos.

Table 1.2: Computer Use from the Quarterly National Householder Survey in March 2001

	August 1998	**September 2000**
Households with Home Computers ('000s)	228.5	416.9
% of all Households	*18.6%*	*32.4%*
% Connected to Internet	*26.8%*	*63.0%*

Parts of inner cities are frequently being described as being *out of control* and the general pressure on teenagers has never been greater. At the other end of the spectrum there is intense competition to get into college due to high demand leading to an intense points race. Some teachers are finding it hard to cope with the modern adolescent and are often quoted as saying that it has never being harder working in the second-level system, such are the demands being placed on them by adolescents.

Ireland has moved rapidly from the economic wilderness to become a wealthy, first-world country. Because of this, there is the possibility of inter-generational conflict. At the same time, there may be greater mobility opportunities and an increased availability of a variety of lifestyle options. These issues may significantly impact on leisure and lifestyle patterns of adolescents.

Chapter 2

SOCIO-ECONOMIC STATUS AND SPORTING ACTIVITY

A primary variable which warrants discussion in any treatise in relation to the process of socialisation into sport is the impact of socio-economic status on leisure activity. Despite the terminological sources of debate that surround the concepts of social class and socio-economic status, there are a number of key conclusions which a search of the literature reveals. These include:

- In all first world countries, middle-class people are considerably more likely to be involved in spare time sporting activities than their working-class counterparts.

- Several sports, including sailing, golf and equestrian sports, are overwhelmingly middle-class activities. There are few activities, with the exceptions of some like boxing, cue sports and darts, which are played more by the working classes.

- Despite the ideological link between sporting ability and social mobility, empirical studies suggest that sport is a means of social mobility for a tiny minority.

This chapter examines the rationale in relation to the effects of social class on sports participation. However, before discussing these, it is first of all necessary to clarify what is meant by social class groupings.

In Ireland, social class distinctions are often thought of as a typically English phenomenon. The popular impression is that the rigid social class demarcation was left behind with the demise of the Anglo-Irish ascendancy. It is true that class boundaries in Ireland are less ritualised or less marked by cultural differences than in some other countries like India and this has encouraged the view that Ireland is, in the main, a classless society. However, there are a wide variety of views in relation to social class in Ireland and writers like Breen and Whelan (1996), in contradicting this assumption, maintain that class barriers in Ireland are in fact substantially more rigid than in other countries. Clare (cited in O'Dea, 1994), on the other hand, claims that apart from the Anglo-Irish ascendancy of the "Big House", there never has been a particularly identifiable and influential Irish upper class. Instead he claims that

> Irish social divisions have been urban and rural, "culchie" and "jackeen", professional and trade, owner/occupier and renter, moneyed and impoverished, educated and unschooled (p. 13).

Social class is one of the most frequently used concepts in sociology and it is also one on which there is considerable divergence of opinion. It is therefore necessary to examine the current definitions of social class.

The primary single indicator of social class grouping normally used is that of occupation (usually of the father). This is somewhat inadequate and sexist. Occupation is not directly equivalent to social class position. There are several other factors that are significant including:

- Factors in relation to property

- Income

- Educational background

- Ability to command resources

- Wealth

- Life chances, defined by Giddens (1973, p. 103) as "the opportunities people have of sharing in the economic and cultural goods which exist in the society".

Therefore, the definition of social class as offered by Giddens encompasses many of the above points. He defines social class as "a large scale group of people who share common economic resources which strongly influence the type of lifestyle which they are able to lead" (1994, p. 24).

Nevertheless, virtually all studies of social class groupings in Ireland use the measure of occupation as the primary determinant of social class. An obvious weakness with any classification based on occupation relates to people outside the workforce. Along with the unemployed (c. 200,000), there are also home workers, the vast majority of whom are women (c. 700,000). Similarly, there are other groups who may not be actively seeking work, e.g. the early retired and people who are on various pensions. There are also significant groups of people who are on government-run job schemes, e.g. the community employment scheme, which had over 40,000 participants in 1997.

A person's life chances, particularly in relation to their sporting and leisure pursuits, may be significantly related to their class position (McPherson et al., 1989; Coakley, 1996; Hendry et al., 1993). There are, however, many critics of class analysis. Clark and Lipset argue that "Social class was the key theme of past stratification work. Yet class is an increasingly outmoded concept" (1991, p. 397). Similarly in Britain, Pahl (1989, p. 710) argues that in modern societies, "class as a concept is ceasing to do any useful work for sociology". The trend in recent years is towards a more disparate family group (Henley Centre, 1987), less inclined to share their meals and leisure time as a household unit but following their own interests (individualisation) and tastes with like-minded peers.

Equally, social class groupings may not act as a gauge of disposable income. A working-class individual may not have a high status job, but may well have more available cash with which to acquire the trappings of society. The financial chains of a large mortgage may be as likely to constrain the higher classes as much as the black economy and overtime may enhance the apparently lower wages of the working classes. In fact, figures from the Department of Social Security in the UK show that the poorest 10 per cent of the population, defined by their income, spend more money than the groups above them in the income distribution class categories.[1] The poorest, who appear to be fully dependent on Social Security benefits, often have their own, informal top-up income.[2]

The variety and complexity of people's jobs make many social classifications inherently subjective rather than objective (O'Brien and Ford, 1989). The debate about the value of analysis by social class groupings was further fuelled when, in August 1987, the British Audience Research Board (BARB) estimated that real changes in social class were likely to be between 4 per cent and 7 per cent per annum. In their view, the middle class was no longer that easily identifiable grouping of people with similar incomes, desires, status and values. An article in *The Sunday Times* showed that in 1979 only 35 per cent of the population in the UK were considered middle class; by 1999, the figure was 50 per cent.[3] This prompted a quote in the same article from Tony Blair, the British Prime Minister, who claimed that the Labour Party "was now the party of the middle classes". These two decades, *The Sunday Times* writer claims, show the biggest shift in class boundaries in 1,000 years.

However, the main problem for critics of class analysis is that, to date, no alternative standard classification variables have been found which have provided consistently better discriminatory powers. Some of the groupings which have been attempted include lifestage groups, Acorn groupings (based on address), attitudinal lifestyle clusters, groups based on possessions and acquisitions and groups based on disposable income (O'Brien and Ford, 1989). Groups have also been based on members' eligibility for certain types of social benefits. Examples here would include people who would be eligible for free school meals in England or for free books and/or medical cards in Ireland.

Goldthorpe and Marshall (1992) provide a defence of class analysis against the critiques of Pahl (1989), Holton and Turner (1994) and Offe (1985). Their defence involves distinguishing class analysis as conducted by those such as Goldthorpe from the class analysis of Marxist sociology. This includes

---

[1] From an article by David Smith in *The Sunday Times*, November 1997.

[2] Ibid.

[3] January 1999.

the interconnections between positions defined by employment relations in labour markets and production units in different sectors of national economies. The processes through which individuals and families are distributed among these positions over time: and the consequences thereof for their life chances and for the social identities they adopt and the social values and interests that they pursue (Goldthorpe and Marshall, 1992, p. 382).

Their view involves neither a theory of history in which class conflict serves as an engine of change, nor a theory of class exploitation. Furthermore, the relationships between class structure, consciousness and action are seen to be contingent.

Most of the Irish research into social class groupings has used categories derived from the census classification of occupations or some other form of prestige ranking. Having reviewed a variety of scales, the one selected as most suitable was Goldthorpe's Social Classification Index. In this scale, seven classes are grouped together under three main groupings:

- Group 1: Professional and Managerial Classes (Classes 1 and 2)

- Group 2: Intermediate Classes (classes 3, 4 and 5)

- Group 3: Working Classes (Classes 6 and 7) (A further classification, namely, class 8: unemployed was added to group 3).

Thus when reviewing literature from different countries, not all the work will be directly comparable, as there are varying classification systems used in different countries. This chapter will therefore present a general picture of the relationship between class and participation in sporting and leisure activities. The findings will be presented under four main headings, which reflect the available research:

- Social mobility

- Barriers to participation

- Economic constraints to participation

- Social class grouping and sport.

SOCIAL MOBILITY

It is certainly possible for athletes from the lower social classes to move up the social class ladder as a result of their sporting endeavours. There are many highly publicised sports people who have done this both in Ireland and across the globe. Roy Keane is a frequently quoted example. He was brought up in a strong working-class area in Cork City. As a teenager, he was on the dole, had left school early and would have been viewed as having few prospects. However, through his soccer ability he went on to become one of the highest paid stars with Manchester United. Thus, there is a powerful ideology which suggests that sport is a major means of social mobility. However, the empirical data, which is American-based, suggests that sport is a means of social mobility only for very small numbers of people. The odds are in fact stacked against any mobility through sport. Coakley (1996) outlines several examples of the small percentage who make it to professional sports in the US. In Table 2.1, for example, he calculates the odds against making it to the pros among high school and college football and basketball players.

Table 2.1: Number of High School Athletes Making Professional Level in the US

	All High School Players	Numbers Making Pros Each Year	Odds Against
Football	947,755	150	6,318 to 1
Basketball	517,271	50	10,345 to 1
Combined	1,465,026	200	7,325 to 1

Source: Coakley, 1996, p. 282.

There are many possible reasons why mobility through sport can be difficult. In many sports, those who aspire to professional or elite amateur status require considerable financial resources in order to fund the required degree of coaching and continual practice. The achievement of elite level status, even for the small minority who achieve this level, would therefore seem to be biased in favour of those from the higher socio-economic groups, especially for sports such as tennis, sailing and golf.

However, even for those who get to college through their sporting endeavours, this sporting prowess by itself is unlikely to lead them to be socially mobile. Stephen Riess in a wide-ranging study in the United States reaches the conclusion that:

> the concept of sport as a vehicle for social mobility is largely a cultural fiction unless young athletes are using sport as the instrument to secure college entrance and complete an education. The great tragedy of the past two decades (70s and 80s) is that few elite athletes be it for lack of preparation, ability or interest are benefiting from their free college education — which is the best means for long term vertical mobility that American sport offers the athletically gifted individual (1990, p. 76).

The reality is that the working classes often reject the middle class school ethos (Hendry, 1978; Lynch, 1989). Bourdieu claims that the education system is "a system of schemes and thoughts and perception . . . which reflects the material and symbolic interests of the dominant groups or classes" (1986, p. 73). Joe Frazier, who came from the black ghettos to win a world heavyweight boxing championship, saw the poor as having lower needs on the Maslowian scale: "education softens a man and that is why the rich can't fight, they will never have to fight to eat".[4]

Eisner and Turner's (1983) study indicated that Olympic participation makes a "marked impact on the future of athletes" (p. 167). However, they remind us that Olympians constitute only a small elite group and that

> for every Olympian, there are thousands of aspiring athletes who never reach the Olympics . . . there are also others who silently recede into the shadows of the ghettos and slums. Their social status, occupational mobility, social mobility, and personal growth would obviously differ from that found to characterise the Olympians. Their stories would perhaps provide us with the human cost of the Olympic Games (p. 171).

---

[4] In a television interview, 1998.

These studies indicate quite clearly that the ideology of social mobility is not supported by the available data on rates of social mobility. The ideology of social mobility through sport does not match the reality.

CLASS BARRIERS TO PARTICIPATION

One of the most obvious barriers to participation in certain sports is the imposition of club membership restrictions. There are a variety of levels of club restrictions. One which appears to be becoming less common is based on gender grounds. For example, Fitzwilliam Lawn Tennis Club in Dublin attracted widespread media and political attention in recent years, and infuriated large segments of the Irish population by consistently refusing, until 1998, full membership to women. One of the reasons for this anger was the perception that many of the club members were in senior social positions or were politically active. A similar situation appears to exist in the Lords Cricket Club in England where women have not even been allowed into certain sections as guests. This gender-differentiated policy had also been widespread within golf clubs but this situation appears to have been changing in recent years. However, when the Irish Open was awarded to Portmarnock Golf Club in 2002, the decision generated considerable controversy, as only men are allowed full membership there.

Golf is one sport which is often seen as being exclusive in nature and it is worth outlining some of the restrictive practices to accessing golf club membership in Ireland. The most obvious restriction is high membership fees. The average norm for initial golf club membership in 1997 was £800 (approximately €1,016).[5] This, plus the annual levy for the first and subsequent years, would be an obvious constraint to a large percentage of the population. Figures quoted by Giddens (1994) show that 50 per cent of English people had savings of £400 or less and thus membership of the average golf club would appear to be financially inaccessible to at least half of the population. Another common restriction is based on approval by election. Even if

---

[5] As outlined in the *Irish Independent* in July 1997.

the prospective entrant has the available cash, they often have to be proposed and seconded by two current members of the club they wish to join. There are other restrictive entry practices that may operate on a local level. One such example, which is still in use in some golf clubs, is the concept of *black balling*. In this instance, each member of a committee assessing a prospective entrant has both a white and a black ball. They vote by placing a white ball for acceptance of the new member or a black ball if they reject the candidate. The voting is anonymous and the committee member does not have to justify their reasoning. If one committee member votes with a black ball, the entrant is refused admission. There are added difficulties for women. Even if they do gain membership, women often do not have voting rights within their club. Where relatively powerful groups have been able to exercise control of this kind, they have often been able to effectively exclude people of relatively modest social backgrounds from club membership and from full participation in certain sports, if they so desire.

The available research would appear to indicate that in most sports the barriers to participation are breaking down and that access to most sports is becoming more widely available (Sage, 1990). The Irish government has indeed endorsed this trend to democratisation. In fact, through equality legislation, introduced in 1999, the Irish government made it illegal for sports clubs to discriminate on the grounds of race, creed or gender. They also made it a requirement for any club which sought lottery funding to have full membership rights for women. However, it is difficult to legislate for private clubs and class barriers do remain in sports such as rugby, tennis, golf, cricket and sailing. Indeed, an indication of the level of perceived discrimination is the fact that a government minister felt it necessary to introduce legislation to counteract the perceived level of discrimination. In these sports, all of which are usually played at private facilities, participants aspire to play with others of a similar social status to their own (McPherson et al., 1989).

There are particular barriers that may be faced by working-class females. There is evidence from the available research of some gender-based class differences in relation to activity levels. Yang, Telamo and Laasko (1996) examined the activity level of 1,881 Finnish boys and girls (nine to fifteen years) over a twelve-year period. Socio-economic status was not associated with the sporting activities of the boys. It was, however, related to the participation of younger girls. Particularly significant differences were revealed between the participation of daughters from high status families and those of low status families, with the former more likely to participate in sport than the latter. Previous research has also identified socio-economic status as one variable that may affect health-related behaviour (Research Unit in Health and Behavioural Change, 1989). More specifically, O'Brien and Ford (1989) suggest that social class is also a strong predicator of health-related behaviour at any given point in time.

ECONOMIC CONSTRAINTS TO SPORTS PARTICIPATION

Economic constraints to participation relate primarily to material resources and the time required in taking part in sport. These factors may limit the degree to which members of differing social classes can take part in different sports. The provision of opportunities for sport and physical recreation has traditionally been regarded as an area suitable for public subsidy (Coalter, 1993). This has been the case for two main reasons. Firstly, there has been a social equity concern to provide equal opportunities for all citizens irrespective of all financial resources (recreational welfare). This is based on an underlying assumption that for many social groups the entrance cost is a major obstacle to participation and that the market would not provide a socially just distribution of opportunities. The second reason is based on the presumed associated functional benefits such as improved health or the reduction in vandalism (Gratton and Taylor, 1988). The available research, however, widely differs in relation to the real effects of cost on participation. Secondary analysis of the 1990/91 General Household Survey by Coalter, Dowers and Baxter (1995) revealed that individuals in higher social classes had higher participation rates in certain sports such as keep-fit, outdoor swimming and golf as compared to the lower social classes. While cost could be assumed to be a factor in relation to golf, this would not be the case in relation to sports such as outdoor swimming. The Audit Commission in the UK (1993) was also critical of the fact that professional people were over-represented in subsidised sports centres.

A study of twelve- and thirteen-year-olds by White and Coakley (1986) found that those children from lower income families cited that the availability of material resources (e.g. transport), specific sports equipment, user/entry fees often acted as economic constraints to their sports participation. They concluded that children from lower income families are not less interested in participating in physical activities but that their participation and their frequency of participation are restricted in comparison to children from higher income families. Other research found that, in particular, entrance fees to leisure centres are not a significant constraint. Coalter's (1993) study of four sports centres and one swimming pool in Scotland found that sports participation is relatively cheap and that constraints to participation are more likely to be related to cultural rather than economic reasons. This study lends support to the work of Kay and Jackson (1991) which illustrated that entrance costs have a low salience as an absolute barrier to participation. In the General Household Survey (1993), only 1 per cent of non-participants referred to the expense of participation as a constraint. Glasgow City Council (1998) carried out a study of two swimming pools, both of which were located in similar disadvantaged areas of Glasgow. To determine the effects of cost on participation, one pool offered free swimming over a six-month period whilst the other charged its regular price. The increased usage in the pool with free swimming was only two per cent with the other pool maintaining its normal level of usage. The results of this study challenged widely held assumptions about the association between sports participation levels and cost.

Cost may or may not be a major factor in local sports facility use. However, it would appear reasonable to conclude that the financial costs associated with certain high cost sports, such as skiing, power-boating and show-jumping for example, would exclude large segments of the population except as spectators. Participants in these sports tend to be drawn from the ranks of the professional or managerial workers. McPherson et al. (1989) have suggested that there is in fact a linear relationship between income and the purchase of sports equipment. By contrast, more easily accessible and less expensive sports such as soccer, Gaelic football, fishing and cycling have a tendency to draw participants from across the class spectrum. The available statistics confirm these points. In the UK, Data from the General Household Surveys confirm data published by the Sports Council's Digest of Sports Statistics (1991). Adults from classes 1 and 2 (professional and managerial employees) dominate the following sports: golf, motor sports, equestrian sports, badminton, rugby, tennis, cricket, squash and yachting. Working-class participants, and particularly those from the upper reaches of the working classes, i.e. skilled manual occupations, are the dominant participants in cue sports, darts, soccer, aerobics and horse-racing (mainly as the punters). Sports which draw participants from across the classes include athletics, angling, cycling and swimming.

SOCIAL CLASS GROUPINGS AND SPORT

Broadly similar research across the world indicate similar results. Studies from the US, Australia, Canada, Belgium, Poland the UK and Germany show that there is an identifiable tendency for non-manual workers and particularly professional and higher managerial workers to take part in sporting activities to a considerably higher degree than do manual workers (McPherson et al., 1989; Gruneau, 1975; Renson, 1976; McKay and Pearson, 1986; Starosta, 1967; Luschen, 1969).

An important factor in sports participation is the availability of time. Sage suggested that one reason why people from the higher social classes tend to participate more in sports is because "they have the leisure time and the money to engage in non-productive activities" (1990, p. 49).

Duffy and Sleap (1982) carried out 583 structured personal interviews with working-class individuals in Ireland to try to establish some of the factors that affect their sports participation. They found an extremely low rate of participation amongst their interviewees. Only 10 per cent claimed that they participated regularly in sport. They found that there were a number of key reasons for their lack of participation:

- A lack of facilities was the most influential reason

- A lack of time due to work or family commitments

- A lack of interest in sport

- Their friends were not taking part.

These four areas will now be discussed.

Many writers are sceptical in relation to non-participants who quote lack of facilities as a reason for non-participation. In many working-class areas, there are in many instances several facilities that attract little usage from the working classes. However, there are a number of critical factors that will also determine if facilities will be used by the working classes other than sheer availability. Goldthorpe et al. (1992), Roberts and Parsell (1991) and West (1988) have shown that the working classes do not normally become involved in the running of an institution. Furthermore, Hargreaves (1980) and Hendry et al. (1993) have observed that the middle classes monopolise social and cultural institutions such as recreational centres. There is also the argument that the facilities provided in working-class areas do not satisfy the needs or wishes of the local population. Kane (1998) gives the example that tennis courts are the second most common outdoor facility provided in the strongly working-class areas of South Dublin County Council. These facilities are widely under-used because the sport is alien to the social world of the people who are expected to use the facilities. He attributes this to the fact that most planners are middle class and as a result they enculturate their own sporting preference onto the working-class recipients of these facilities. Given these facts, it may not be surprising that the working classes are not attracted to organisations or activities that promote the values of another subculture.

Similar scepticism is expressed in relation to the question of time being a problem. The average working-class person may spend up to 25 hours per week watching television. This evidence presents an obvious contradiction. One argument that has been put forward here is that family commitments in the working-class household can be fulfilled while the television is on. Family obligation can be particularly restrictive on working-class women. Their middle-class counterparts may be able to afford childcare and will probably have fewer children. The working-class "captive wife" as identified by Gavron (1966) may still be a contributing factor to lack of time for working-class women. However, there is a clear argument that for many the time is available but they choose non-sport activities during this free time. Coakley throws another angle on this topic when he says:

> People from lower income groups often spend so much of their time and energy coping with the challenges of everyday life that they have no energy left for sports, even when sports are free and accessible (1996, p. 277).

There is also a theoretical view that the whole ethos of sport may be alien to working-class attitudes. An early proponent of this view was Luschen (1970) who stated that

> the higher social classes have a culture of their own, the greatest emphasis is on achievement, and thus the highest sports participation is to be found in the upper middle class. It is considerably less important in the lower class where routine responsibility is valued (p. 231).

Luschen further suggested that because sports clubs were central to the organisation of sport and because members of the working class were apprehensive about joining formal club organisations, this was effectively a barrier that often turned the working classes away from sport. This view was evident in a major study conducted in Britain in 1960 by the Central Council for Physical Recreation (CCPR). This study showed that the working classes were by and large not particularly interested in participating in major team games outside compulsory schooling. Hargreaves (1986) claims that this pattern of non-conformity continued to be a feature of the responses of sections of the working classes to participation in organised physical recreation well beyond the 1960s.

A further important point is in relation to social relationships. Goldthorpe and Marshall (1992) in their study of working-class lifestyles showed that manual workers were less interested in developing social relationships with white-collar workers and "tended to follow a family centred and relatively privatised pattern of social life" (p. 42). As well as suggesting this as a possible reason for the high consumption of television, their argument suggests that if the middle class already dominate sports clubs and facilities, the working class may not be keen to break into that particular way of life. This theory could also explain why, if a sports facility is located in a working class area but exhibits middle-class characteristics in both the way it is managed and the class of the users, it may easily fail to attract widespread working-class usage. Since sports participation mainly demands outgoing and group-oriented qualities, participation in many sports would seem to run contrary to the privatised way of life favoured by manual workers.

The influence of friends and their interests will often determine the leisure interests of the average person. Christensen and Youesting (1978) gave significant prominence to the effects of social networks in determining leisure behaviour claiming that "an individual's use of recreation facilities is related to his personal communities or the influence of his family, friends, work mates or relatives" (p. 22). Veal (1994) describes this as a person's "mental map". McPherson et al. (1989) found, more than any other factor, that an individual is strongly influenced in their sports participation by another member of the family, usually the father. Lamon (1977) in his research concluded that the most significant predictor of whether sport is practised or not lies in the education of the father. The longer the father remained in education, the more likely it is that the child will take part in sport. Because the working-class father is more likely to have left school earlier than his middle-class counterpart, the working-class child is less likely to be encouraged into sport. Indifferent or negative attitudes and values to sports participation are passed on from working-class parents to their children and thus the cycle of inactivity continues.

It would thus appear that the legacy that remains is a sporting ethos which is still permeated by middle-class values and which is still more alien to working-class lifestyles. Sport remains uninviting for many working-class individuals. The middle classes on the other hand are more involved (time) and are also involved in a wider variety of activities than the working classes. The research also clearly points to the fact that those social structures or classes may not only contain human behaviours but may also influence human behaviour. Haralambos and Holborn summarise this view when they state that "people choose to engage in leisure pursuits which fit in with their personal circumstances, lifestyle and the social groups to which they belong" (1995, p. 256).

The following quote from the Miller Lite study of sport in the US also reflects the general consensus to the effect of socioeconomic status on sport as reflected in the available literature:

> Who plays, who watches and who consumes information about sports is clearly connected with class relations in all societies, involvement in and with sports goes hand and hand with money, power and privilege (Miller Lite Report, 1983).

Beamish summarises the actual impact when he says:

> People in high income and high status occupational groups have the highest rates of active participation, the highest rates of attendance at sports events and even the highest viewing rates for sports on TV (1990, p. 143).

Finally, Hargreaves encapsulates the relationship between social class and sport participation when he says:

> We can dismiss the idea that sports nowadays embourgeoisify the working class . . . involvement in sport, whatever section of the class we consider, does not induce an identification with, or facilitate mixing with bourgeois elements or lead to the adoption of a bourgeois lifestyle . . . we know the middle and upper classes effectively place obstacles in the way of the lower classes mixing with them in sporting activity. We also know that working class people on the whole do not aspire to join them (1986, p. 111).

Chapter 3

THE EFFECTS OF SCHOOLING AND PHYSICAL EDUCATION ON SPORT AND LEISURE ACTIVITY

There is a general consensus in the available literature which examines the impact of school type on sport and leisure participation. Up to the 1950s in the UK and into the 1960s in Ireland, there were two main traditions with significantly different attitudes towards sports provision in the second-level school system. These were the public and private schools in the UK and the secondary and vocational schools in Ireland. Since then, there has been a general democratisation within this area but there are still some discrepancies. There are strong historical reasons for the two traditions: particularly in England, the influence of the games ethic within public schools was significant and this has impacted on the subsequent development of sport. This is the first area which will be discussed. The impact of the school on gender stereotyping will then be examined as many of the stereotypes that currently influence adolescents result from historical developments within the educational system. The development of Irish education and how this has influenced sporting provision will then be explored. The final section examines the current state of physical education and sports provision in Irish schools.

THE GAMES ETHIC IN THE ENGLISH PUBLIC SCHOOL SYSTEM

The development of what became known as the "games ethic" evolved in parallel to the industrial revolution in the UK. Kirk (1990) describes this evolution (c.1850):

> The cult of athleticism and its accompanying Games Ethic
> were born in the Public Schools of the male bourgeois classes
> in Victorian Britain, and formed a powerful political ideology
> that was to become influential well beyond the boundaries of
> space, time, nationality and social class (p. 180).

The public schools were seen to serve a number of purposes for the bourgeois males. On the one hand, schools were a vehicle of social mobility but on the other they also sought to preserve and promote exclusiveness. The advent of the industrial revolution had brought profound changes to English society. There were massive population shifts leading to intensive urbanisation. There was also a new wealthy and powerful middle class who emerged from this upheaval, who wanted to consolidate their place in the social hierarchy at levels which reflected their members' material wealth. Kirk (1990) maintains that reforming the public school system and including within it a cult of athleticism was central to ensuring their privileged place in society.

The games ethic within the public schools system was instituted for a number of key reasons. As well as satisfying leisure needs, games were perceived as a means of disciplining and normalising the male youths of the ruling classes (Mangan, 1983). The games ethic came to express the "quintessential bourgeois English qualities that were felt to make the English superior to foreigners" (Hargreaves, 1986, p. 75). There was a belief that games promoted both expressive and instrumental qualities. In particular, team games were felt to promote loyalty, self-control, perseverance, fairness and courage, both moral and physical (Mangan, 1983). A number of clichés from this period used in common parlance today reflect the perceived importance of the games ethic at the time. These include "it's not cricket", "play the game" and the "Napoleonic wars were won on the playing fields of Eton". All of these sayings give an indication of the lasting importance that the games ethic fostered within the psyche of the public school system. By 1870, Mangan argues that the cult of athleticism began to be imitated by other sections of the bourgeoisie:

> The evolution of the Grammar Schools involved, in large
> measure, imitation of its upper class superiors and segrega-

tion from its working class inferiors . . . the differential absorption of the athletic mores of the Public Schools reveals a significant hegemonic process at work (1983, p. 313).

In stark contrast, team games were not considered suitable for the working class: a grouping of people whose destiny was to follow rather than lead. Instead of games, a form of drill was introduced for them into state elementary schools in the late nineteenth century. The state was adopting a functionalist rationale as they wanted to maintain a fit, disciplined and healthy population that could be mobilised at times of war (McIntosh, 1959). Drill was then incorporated as a recognised subject into the payments by results scheme that was operational at the time.

It was not until after the First World War that the cult of athleticism began a long and gradual decline in influence within the male public school system. By 1944, the Butler Education Act saw the introduction of second-level schooling for all and the school-going age was increased to fifteen in 1947. This led to the growth of mass education, which was also accompanied by an increasing physical education profession that helped democratise sports provision within the education system. Hargreaves (1986) identified three main forces that were instrumental in bringing about a rise in the prominence of games in government second-level schools:

1. The first was the increasing state intervention in sport and recreation outside the school system. This soon began to draw school and community physical education and recreation into the state's sphere of interest.

2. Competitive games and sports came to be seen as a unifying force and a means of promoting national identity.

3. A third factor that boosted the fortunes of competitive sports and games in schools was the concern for social order, particularly in relation to working class youth and their use of leisure time. Games were perceived as providing a cathartic outlet for youthful energy and kept potential troublemakers busy.

Games and sport did not form a significant part of the school physical education programme in the state sector until the late 1940s. Soon afterwards, competitive team sports became the core of the physical education programme. Kirk documents this dramatic change and the move towards democratisation:

> During the decade and a half following the Second World War, a version of physical education that until the 1950s had been traditional to elite private schools in Britain became traditional physical education for everyone, for the masses as well as the socially and economically deprived (1990, p. 142).

The games ethic in Britain has thus experienced the *embourgeoisement* process. Team games occupied a central role in the education of bourgeois males from the mid-eighteenth century. Toward the end of the 1800s, upper-class women and other less wealthy members of the bourgeoisie took up games. It was the late 1940s before games-playing dominated the physical education curricula for the masses and this situation has continued to this day.

SCHOOL GENDER STEREOTYPING AND PHYSICAL EDUCATION — A HISTORICAL ANALYSIS

To gain an understanding of the factors which may lead to gender stereotyping in physical education and games, it is important to examine how this stereotyping evolved by examining it from a historical perspective. School stereotyping in relation to physical education and games has a long history. From the end of the nineteenth century, the games ethic began to dominate the physical education syllabus of bourgeois girls' schools in much the same manner as happened in the boys' schools. However, the games that were played were different and the same excesses did not apply. Games such as netball and lacrosse were introduced to girls' schools in the 1880s and 1890s:

> These activities emphasised the co-operative and therapeutic aspects of play rather than the physically vigorous and competitive character of the male games (Kirk, 1990, p. 120).

While in the wider social context sport was part of an emancipatory movement for upper-class women, challenging notions of the delicate female constitution and other mores concerning clothing and display of the body, games-playing in the girls' schools was still framed within patriarchal notions of women and motherhood (Hargreaves, 1985). Women were not expected to become leaders in politics, the military or business, and so the characteristics and values that marked the male ethos were seen as unnecessary for females (McCrone, 1988). Whilst participation by women in sport led to greater freedoms for some, old ideas died hard. McIntosh quotes a letter from one Miss Conroy (a high school headmistress), published in *The Lancet* in 1922, which stated that

> eighty per cent of gymnastics teachers had breakdowns, that playing strenuous games developed a flat figure with underdeveloped breasts, that athletic women suffered from nerves, heart trouble, rheumatism, suppressed menstruation and displacements, that they decried marriage, that their confinements were always difficult, that their children were often inferior, and that most athletic women seemed to have stifled what is finest in women — love, sympathy, tact and intuitive understanding (1959, p. 23).

This kind of view would appear to have been enough to make games-playing less popular with girls than boys.

Another unique feature to girls' schools was that for many years they were taught by a professional body of female physical education teachers. In the boys' schools, it was expected as part of a normal teacher's repertoire that he would teach games (McIntosh, 1959). A similar situation existed in Ireland. Whilst there were two PE courses exclusively for women,[1] it was not until 1973 that a male could train to be a PE teacher in Ireland. This coincided with the establishment of the National College of Physical Education in Limerick. This may reflect a societal bias about the masculine nature of most sports as alluded to above by McIntosh. In the UK, games such as netball were in the

---

[1] The first of these colleges, Ling Physical Training College, was founded in 1900. Numbers attending the college averaged about twenty per year.

female teacher-training curriculum in the 1880s with gymnastics forming the core of the professional educator's art until the end of the Second World War. Two things happened at this time which were influential: firstly, the 1944 Butler Education Act; and secondly, there was an influx of males into the physical education profession in the post-war period.

This introduction of second-level education for all and the raising of the school-leaving age presented a considerable challenge for the government in the UK. There were the added costs of new school buildings, improved facilities and the necessary staff to fulfil the terms of the legislation. Physical educators were faced with the challenge of adapting their practices with new limitations both in terms of a lack of facilities and teachers, and a new mass of older pupils who, unlike their grammar school peers, encompassed a wider range of academic and physical abilities. General changes in the teaching of physical education were soon noted:

> The report in 1946 of a survey of physical education in girls' Secondary schools showed that games and gymnastics dominated the curriculum, with little time for dancing, swimming or athletics (*The Leaflet*, 1946, p. 123).

The new male entrants to the physical education profession are acknowledged to have been primarily responsible for the rise in dominance of games on the PE curriculum (Kirk, 1990). Whilst competitive sport had formed a part of the female tradition since its establishment, there was a consistent policy of opposition to over-competitiveness. The Ling Association, in particular, followed a consistent policy of opposition to over-competitiveness from the late 1800s up to the 1940s. They displayed on the one hand an open antagonism towards the excesses of the male public school tradition, and on the other an appreciation and support for a distinctive bourgeois female approach to games and sports (McIntosh, 1959). Hargreaves (1994) has interpreted the enthusiasm for games-playing among male physical educators in two ways. Firstly, she sees this appropriation of games as an extension of competitive sport and games in general. Secondly, her view is that the female physical educators were, with few exceptions, from the privileged strata of British society.

Male physical educators, on the other hand, tended to be drawn from the lower end of the social class spectrum and their social and professional status in the 1940s and 1950s was certainly inferior to that of women. By the end of the 1960s, significant changes were evident as a result of the changing nature of the physical education profession. Two major surveys, including one from the Central Council for Physical Recreation in 1960, showed the decline of gymnastics. It rated a mention but was only popular amongst a very small number of pupils. Secondly, whilst there is clear domination by games, the games played were stereotyped — soccer, rugby and cricket for boys, netball and hockey for girls — while athletics was the only major activity where participation rates straddled the two sexes. It could be argued, therefore, that there was over time a subtle imposition of traditional male games onto the school curriculum.

The difficulties of changing these stereotypical images are addressed by many authors. Armstrong (1994a) has outlined the importance of encouraging girls to become more active and of the need for schools to make this a priority. Gender ideologies and behaviours are apparent in the infant age group and the school has been identified as one of the primary socialisation agents (McPherson et al., 1989; Greendorfer and Lewko, 1988) of gender behaviour for health-related sports participation. A survey by the Physical Education Association in the UK (1987) showed that the heads of physical education departments regarded health-related fitness as the second most important objective but their curricula often did not reflect this emphasis. The hidden curriculum of schools shows that games dominate the curriculum and that, while the PE heads may espouse the values of other areas, this does not carry over into what actually happens on the ground. The hidden curriculum may also reflect the relative value given to male as opposed to female sports. This is an issue that is taken up by Armstrong (1994a). Within school sport, girls' games such as hockey and netball appear to carry less prestige than boys' games such as rugby and soccer. This may reinforce the relative unimportance of physical activity in the lives of women and young girls. The dominance of boys' games in the social life of the school may reinforce the ideology of domination of women by men (Armstrong, 1994).

THE IRISH SITUATION

From the literature available, it does not appear that the Irish education system has ever come under the same influence of the games ethic as appears to have been the case within the public school system in England. The main significant difference in Ireland has been the historically dominant influence by the Catholic Church on second-level education. An interesting illustration of this relationship and its effect on physical education in Ireland is documented by Noel Browne in his book *Against the Tide*, where he quotes a fascinating letter from the hierarchy to the Taoiseach of the day:

> The right to provide for the physical education of children belongs to the family and not to the State. Experience has shown that physical or health education is closely interwoven with important moral questions on which the Catholic Church has definite teaching (1986, p. 158).

There are, however, a number of broad similarities, with an apparent time-lag between events in Britain and similar such developments in Ireland. The Department of Education was set up in 1924, following the establishment of Saorstát Éireann. An early report by the Department alluded to the sectarian nature of physical education in Irish schools:

> Public schools offered cricket. Christian Brothers' schools, hurling, football. In girls' schools in particular, drill was popular with instructors from local barracks (1925, pp. 24–25).

Within Irish education at this period, there were two main streams of educational provision. The vocational sector, which was state-run, and the secondary education system, which was outside the ambit of state control. These two streams of educational provision will now be examined, followed by a brief look at later developments in Irish educational provision.

Secondary Education

Early Irish secondary education came under the pervasive influence of the Church. While the state made several attempts to get more involved, Coolahan states that "there was perennial opposition on the part of churches in Ireland to state encroachment on secondary school management" and, in fact, it "was not until 1964 that the first state grant was given for capital expenditure on secondary schools" (1985, p. 53).

Many of the secondary schools were diocesan schools, which were seen as formative schools for future clergy, and the participation rates in secondary education by the Irish public were low in the early years of the Irish Republic. The schools, however, became more popular, as can be seen from the enrolment figures in Table 3.1.

Table 3.1: Expansion of Secondary Education in Ireland, 1924–80

Year	No. of Secondary Schools	No. of Students
1924/5	278	22,897
1930/1	300	28,994
1940/1	352	38,713
1950/1	424	48,559
1960/1	526	76,843
1978/9	531	96,606

Source: Coolahan, 1985, p. 79; Dept of Education, 1980.

Coolahan outlined how secondary education was the preserve of the ruling classes:

> Secondary schooling conducted in private, fee-paying institutions was seen as a middle class concern. It was the professional and merchant classes of the towns and established tenant farmers who aimed at giving their children the benefit and prestige of a secondary education . . . [whilst] the poor and the working classes were largely seen by leaders of the Church and State as a self-perpetuating section of so-

ciety for whom a limited education of literacy and numeracy was deemed sufficient (1985, p. 55).

The curriculum of the secondary schools was firmly fixed within the humanist grammar school tradition and there is scant mention of sport in any literature regarding secondary education in the early years. However, due to a geographical imbalance in the provision of schools, a boarding school tradition became strongly established and Coolahan (1985) recounts that, as late as 1944, one-third of all secondary school pupils were in boarding schools. The traditions of secondary schools were firmly rooted on both sectarian and gender segregation. Each school usually catered for only one religion and one gender. Sport was in general limited to extra-curricular provision and was generally absent from the daily school curriculum.

Vocational Education

As the name implies, this strand of educational provision in Ireland has aimed at fulfilling the vocational and technical needs of the country. This philosophy is firmly rooted in an early commission which was established in 1926 by the Department of Education to "enquire into and advise upon the system of technical education in Saorstát Éireann in relation to Trade and Industry" (Report on the Commission on Technical Education, 1928, p. 12).

The recommendations of this commission led to the Vocational Education Act of 1930. Two broad elements were incorporated into vocational education in this act, namely, continuing and vocational education. The vocational schools would be funded by local rates and there was an onus to provide schools in all areas of the country. The schools were under secular control and were non-denominational in nature. Vocational education was perceived as a different type of education to secondary education. Coolahan aptly describes this:

> In reply to a deputation from the Catholic Hierarchy, the Minister for Education was at pains to assure them in a written reply that continuing education did not involve "general education" and was to be severely practical and vocational in its emphasis (1985, p. 97).

It is interesting to note that there was no mention of physical education and/or games on the curriculum in vocational schools. With the assistance of state funding after the new act, there was strong growth in the provision of vocational schools, as can be seen in Table 3.2:

Table 3.2: Growth in Number of Vocational Schools

Year	No of Vocational Schools
1921	65
1936	111
1993	244

However, these schools were curtailed in the type of curriculum that they could provide. It was not until 1966 that the government decided to abolish the academic/technical divide by raising the status of vocational schools. Vocational schools were only then able to offer the full cycle of second-level education.

Comprehensive Schools, Community Schools and Community Colleges

The dual provision of education continued for the first 40 years of the Irish state's existence and the government was keen to address this issue by the 1960s. Crooks and McKiernan outline two main reasons for the Government's way of thinking:

1. The lack of educational facilities in some parts of the country.

2. The fact that secondary and vocational education were being conducted as separate entities with no connecting link between them (1984, p. 5).

By 1966, the first comprehensive schools were in operation with state funding. Their intention was to pool educational resources so that a full range of academic subjects could be offered. Coolahan states in relation to comprehensive schools that they were "mostly co-educational and no selection occurred at entry. The state built and funded the comprehensive schools

completely" (1985, p. 143). Their management structure comprised management boards with representatives of different
interest groups, including the Church and the local authority.

In 1970, the pulling-together of the two educational strands
was further strengthened by the establishment of the community schools, which were set up to provide a comprehensive-
type education with no entry restrictions based on the pupil's
academic ability. There was also a strong emphasis on estab-
lishing links between the school and the local community by
aiming to make the school's facilities available to the community. The Department of Education owns these schools.

The Vocational Education Committees were worried about
the erosion of their power because of the strong growth in the
provision of community and comprehensive schools. The VECs
had strong political representation and as a result of their lobbying, there were no more comprehensive schools built after
1974. A Vocational Education Amendment Act was passed in
1970 which led to the emergence of the community colleges.
These were similar to community schools but were under the
control of the Vocational Education Committees.

Thus there are currently five types of second-level schools
in Ireland. However, the secondary schools are still the key
players, as can be seen in Table 3.3:

**Table 3.3: Attendance at Second-Level Schools in the Republic
of Ireland 1993/4**

Category	No. of Students	% of total
Secondary Schools	224, 035	61%
Vocational Schools	94,760	26%
Community Schools/Colleges	39,487	11%
Comprehensive Schools	9,363	3%
Total	367,645	

Source: *Irish Almanac and Yearbook of Facts*, 1997, p. 177.

Having briefly examined the development of the different school types in Ireland, the next section will examine the current state of sport in Irish schools.

SPORT IN IRISH SCHOOLS

Whilst there has been a strong democratisation towards the provision of sport in Ireland, there are still discrepancies, many of them historical. For instance, if a school had sporting facilities, it is likely that they would have been predisposed towards providing physical education and sports classes. Similarly, during the 1980s there was a government embargo on providing new jobs in the public sector in Ireland. Therefore, if a school had no physical education teachers, it was extremely difficult to get the Department to sanction such an appointment during this period. The building of sports facilities is still not mandatory. Therefore, many schools have to fundraise extensively and lobby through political means for their sports facilities. Even then, in some instances, there can be the added problem of not having available space to build facilities or to provide sports grounds.

The Department of Education has recommendations both in relation to the amount of physical education each student is expected to receive and to the type of facilities which are stipulated as being necessary (PE Syllabus, 1988). For instance, pupils are expected to have two hours of physical education per week for each year that they are in school. The facilities that are considered necessary include suitable indoor spaces, outdoor playing areas, access to swimming pools and outdoor pursuits areas. However, the situation on the ground appears to be at variance with the recommendations of the Department. Similarly, as the following tables show, there are significant variations between school types and the provision of sports and physical education.

The situation at junior cycle level, as illustrated in Figure 3.1 below, would appear to indicate that physical education is given a lower priority at junior cycle level in vocational schools (71 per cent) when compared to other school types which have higher levels of provision (92 per cent).

Figure 3.1: Number of Pupils Taking Junior Cycle PE

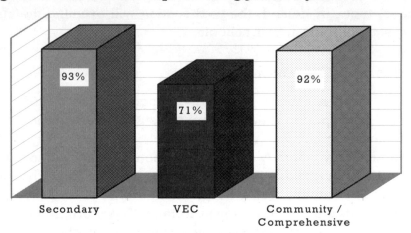

Source: Dept. of Education, Statistical Report, 1989.

The position is considerably exacerbated at senior cycle level, as can be seen from the Figure 3.2 below. Whilst all schools show lower provision at this level, which in itself is an interesting indicator of the perceived values which schools place on PE, the provision in vocational schools is under half (44 per cent). In terms of curricular provision for physical education, it would appear that the secondary schools and the community and comprehensive schools are placing almost equal emphasis, through their time allocation, on physical education provision.

Figure 3.2: Number of Pupils Taking Senior Cycle PE

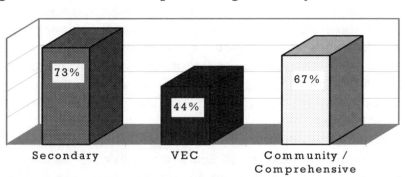

Source: Dept. of Education Statistical Report, 1989.

In relation to the availability of an indoor sports hall, the community/comprehensive schools are the clear leaders in providing these facilities, as shown in Figure 3.3 below. There are a number of possible reasons for this, which are not necessarily based on curricular issues. Firstly, these are the newer schools, all of which have been built since the 1960s. As the government of the time had developed a policy of investment in education, they had an increased chance of funding. Secondly, these schools are generally bigger than the average secondary school and, in many instances, would have involved amalgamations of a number of smaller schools. As a result, they would have had more lobbying power when requesting sports facilities. It is interesting to note that the vocational school sector is not lagging far behind the secondary school sector in the provision of indoor sports facilities. Even though the level of provision of indoor facilities appears to be equal in both sectors, the provision levels for PE in secondary schools are so much higher that this indicates that there are a higher number of PE teachers working in this sector. Whilst the levels of facility provision are almost level, the level of staff resources for the vocational sector lags behind the secondary sector.

Figure 3.3: Second Level Schools with an Indoor Sports Facility

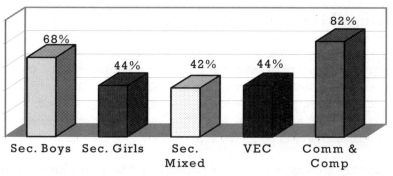

Source: Dept. of Ed. Statistical Report, 1989

Deenihan (1991) carried out a survey of all second-level schools in Ireland in relation to PE provision and also on the value placed on PE within the curriculum. He received a reply rate of 62 per cent and even though his survey may have been politically motivated, the results of the survey make interesting reading.[2] He found that:

- 42 per cent of second level schools were not offering physical education at senior cycle.

- The student/PE teacher ratio was 534:1. This compares with 250:1 in Britain, the US and Australia.

- 28 per cent of schools surveyed had no PE teacher.

- 26 per cent of schools had no facilities, not even a large classroom.

- Ireland was the only country in the European Union that did not have compulsory PE for second-level students.

Whilst Deenihan did not break down his results based on school type, Lynch (1989) did so and she was definitive in outlining the differing provision levels of facilities in the differing school types. Interestingly, her figures contradict official figures given by the Department of Education. She found that:

> Only 22 per cent of vocational schools had gym facilities of their own compared with 67 per cent of secondary schools, and 80 per cent of community schools (pp. 113–114).

Furthermore, in relation to playing fields:

> Vocational schools have poorest provision of any school type, 19 per cent of them have no playing fields whilst a further 41 per cent rely on renting one. This means that only 40 per cent have playing fields of their own compared with 74 per cent of secondary and 70 per cent of community/ comprehensive schools (p. 112).

Even in the area of hard court provision, there are clear differences:

---

[2] Jimmy Deenihan qualified as a PE teacher and later entered the Dáil as a Fine Gael deputy for Kerry North.

> One-third of vocational schools have no hard court, whilst 19 per cent of secondary schools have no hard court. All community schools had courts of their own (p. 113).

Thus, it would appear clear that the level of provision for physical education is poorer in vocational schools, and that PE is marginalised and on the periphery of the curriculum for a significant number of secondary schools. The Department of Education, while appearing to advocate the teaching of PE, shows a distinct lack of will to push the subject to the core of curriculum provision. Left to localised decision by individual schools, the current situation shows a bias towards higher provision both in terms of facilities and time allocation in the secondary as opposed to the vocational sector. However, this appears by no means to be clear-cut and may be subject to many locally determined factors. There are several vocational schools with better provision levels than some of their secondary counterparts. The clear link between the games ethic and the public school system in England has not been mirrored in the Irish education system. The secondary school system historically has provided a humanistic academic education and the vocational schools have provided a technical/vocational education. Sport and physical education have been side issues along the way. In recent years, the curricula of both sectors appear to have become more uniform. However, there are still clear differences in the provision levels particularly between the vocational and other sectors and this is likely to impact on the participation levels of the adolescents attending these schools.

PHYSICAL ACTIVITY LEVELS OF IRISH STUDENTS

The current level of physical activity amongst Irish children appears to be a cause for concern. By the end of their second-level schooling, fewer than half of Irish adolescents are taking PE. Girls appear to be less active than boys while participation levels in physical activity by both genders decline as they move through the second-level education system (Watson, 1990a; 1990b). Physical educators may be the best placed to foster more active lifestyles through the promotion of "knowledge and understanding of the beneficial effects of health related physical activity and the ways in which these benefits can be achieved and sustained" (Agreed Aim of British Association of Sport Sciences, Health Education Authority and British Physical Education Association, 1990).

Research indicates (Sallis and Patrick, 1994) that, in general, physical education does not provide adequate amounts of physical activity to meet the physical activity guidelines set down for adolescents. These data also suggest that substantial numbers of adolescents and the majority of girls are not sufficiently active. The gender differences in physical activity suggest that effective intervention is necessary, particularly for girls. During adolescence, time spent by both girls and boys in physical activity declines and the decline continues into adulthood (Hendry et al., 1993). Because of this downward trend, even those adolescents currently meeting the physical activity guidelines are at risk of becoming sedentary adults (Sallis and Patrick, 1994). There may be class-linked issues to these participation rates. In reference to young children and adolescents, Hendry (1978) pointed out that academically successful students often fuse school life with leisure while educational failures, who are mainly from the working classes, separate these two spheres totally. These factors are likely to impact on the levels of participation in sport by Irish working-class adolescents.

In summary, it would appear that school provision for sport and PE is not rooted in a firm foundation and would appear to be determined by several factors, not necessarily curricular in nature. The games ethic has left behind a tradition where team games dominate the sports curricula of schools. Similarly, male sports appear to have been imposed on girls. These factors may be directly linked to a number of the reasons why adolescent girls in particular drop out of sport; the impact of gender will be addressed in more detail in the next chapter.

Chapter 4

GENDER AND SPORT AND LEISURE PARTICIPATION

The focus in the literature in relation to gender and sport generally portrays the inequalities that exist in the sporting experiences of females as opposed to males. Both qualitative and quantitative studies (Mason, 1995; Kremer et al., 1997; Hendry et al., 1993) consistently show that women have less leisure time, take part in a narrower range of sporting activities, are more home-based in their leisure and use a more limited range of sporting locations than their male counterparts.

There has been a considerable volume of research carried out in this area since the 1950s. Allied to the increasing growth of the feminist movement across the world since then, sports participation by women has increasingly come under the spotlight. Researchers have attempted to establish women's patterns of involvement in sporting and leisure activities. Many have specifically investigated the extent of, and reasons for, women's participation in particular sports and, conversely, their lack of participation in other sports. Early investigations in the 1960s maintained that games and sports involving physical skill were negatively associated with the female sex role (Moss and Kagan, 1961). However, Landers and Luschen (1970) pointed out that at this stage sports were becoming increasingly available to women in our society.

Compared to male participation, there was a wide inequality in a number of key areas. Smith and Harrison (1987) analysed national surveys conducted in the 1970s and 1980s in the US, Canada, East Germany, Norway and other European countries. They found consistent results across these countries. A paraphrase of their findings showed that:

- Men participate more regularly (in terms of time spent and percentage engaging in an activity) in more active and vigorous sport and recreation;

- Women tend to be participate more than men in certain less active, less vigorous and less dangerous sports and recreational activities.

The same general trends can be found in adolescent boys and girls. Several studies have found that boys were more active than girls (Blair et al., 1989; Armstrong and Biddle, 1990; Verschuur and Kemper, 1985; Ross et al., 1985; Butcher and Hall, 1983; Wales Sports Council, 1987; Northern Ireland Fitness Survey, 1989). Thirlaway and Benton (1993) found, in a study of 684 West Glamorgan schoolchildren, that boys were more active than girls. They reasoned that this was principally because they played more team games than girls. There may also be gender differences in the types of activity participated in by girls and boys. Verschuur and Kemper (1985) and Kremer et al. (1997) reported that boys spent more time in *heavy* (e.g. rugby) physical activities whereas girls spent more time on *light* (e.g. swimming) physical activities. Dunning (1983) attributes these differences to the gender socialisation process when he said that "young girls are encouraged to believe that competitive and recreational sport is trivial and is something that their brothers do" (p. 12).

This chapter aims, therefore, to examine gender socialisation and investigate the reasons why boys and girls participate (or not) in different activities and at different levels. Secondly, this chapter will also explore why the socialisation agencies within society lead to greater status being accorded to boys' activities than to those of girls. Taking an overview of the available literature and research as a whole, the following factors appear to influence females and their participation levels in sport and leisure:

1. Traditional ideas of femininity

2. Homophobia in women's sport and physical education

3. Perpetuation of traditional stereotypes

4. The influence of significant others

5. The family

6. The socialisation process

7. The mass media.

TRADITIONAL IDEAS OF FEMININITY

Szali et al. (1973) carried out early work on multinational research in the form of a time budget survey. From their research, the results from twelve countries were compared. They detected a strong bias in women's leisure time orientation towards activities that corresponded to traditional ideas of femininity. Another key finding from their research was that women were themselves responsible for prolonging stereotyped, traditional ideas about their own roles and identities.

Cahn (1994) highlighted the fact that while the feminist movement had questioned basic assumptions about the place of women in various social institutions, this movement had not concerned itself with the whole issue of equality for women in the sports arena. She maintained that the feminist movement had done nothing to prevent the traditional stereotyped ideas being prolonged. Talbot (1979), in reviewing North American literature concerning women and sport, also felt that this tended to reflect a prevailing anxiety about sex roles and femininity. Participation by women and their achievements in physical activities was perceived to threaten conceptions about both masculine and feminine behaviour.

Metheny (1965) studied the whole issue of the social acceptability of women athletes in the 1960s. She found variations in the acceptability of different types of athletic participation. Some aspects of competition in particular were considered less acceptable for women and these included:

• Bodily contact with an opponent

• Application of force with some heavy object

• Projecting the body through space over long distances

- Co-operative face-to-face competition.

She also found the converse to be true, i.e. that there were aspects of competition which were more acceptable and thus less contradictory to the female role. These included:

- Presenting the body in aesthetically pleasing patterns

- Use of a manufactured device to facilitate body movement

- Use of a light implement and/or light object as in tennis or badminton

- Maintenance of a spatial barrier with an opponent (paraphrased from Deem, 1986).

Further credence to the suggestion that traditional ideas of the female role influence women's participation is given by McPherson et al. (1989) in their discussion on gender role conflict. Their treatise states that the female competitor must ultimately decide whether to fulfil her socially sanctioned ascribed female role or to ignore these norms and achieve her full potential in sport. The females who persist may be labelled as deviant and stigmatised as being masculine or manly. They may be called tomboys or other age-appropriate epithets.

Sharon Mathes (1978) found that athletes report across sports a preoccupation with their appearance. They were concerned with avoiding the masculinisation of the body that many female athletes feel is an inevitable consequence of sports participation. This sentiment is echoed in a quotation by Vicki Foltz, one of America's finest long-distance runners:

> a lot of us try, subconsciously maybe, to look as feminine as possible in a race. It is because so many people have said that women athletes look masculine (quoted in Mathes, 1978, p. 66).

Hargreaves (1994) and Deem (1986) both point to the dissonance experienced by the female athlete. They both suggest that the female athlete, as a result of being an asocial anomaly, may attempt to emphasise her femininity whilst expressing a strong commitment to sports participation. This may take the form of dressing in gender-appropriate ways, not taking sports seriously, pursuing the so-called more acceptable sports, underachieving in sport to maintain peer group popularity or in any way reaffirming the feminine values of their society.

The existence of traditional ideas of femininity and traditional ideas of the female role has had serious ramifications for the female athlete. The Olympic movement has historically placed barriers as to what sports could be contested by women. This situation has recently improved, as demonstrated by the motto of the Atlanta Olympics that named the 1996 Games the Olympics for Women.[1] However, even today, there are restrictions on certain women's events. Obvious examples would include the steeplechase, pole vault and boxing. McPherson et al. (1989) claim that many sports, including wrestling, football and ice hockey, are deemed inappropriate for women. Many women are therefore limited in their participation in sporting activities by socially accepted norms and preconceived notions of what is appropriate and also by what is felt to be humanly possible to achieve. A particularly important constraint to women's participation in sport may be homophobic attitudes and this topic will now be discussed.

HOMOPHOBIA IN WOMEN'S SPORT AND PHYSICAL EDUCATION

An analysis of homophobia in women's sport and physical education is of importance for two main reasons. Firstly, there is the fear that being labelled lesbian or gay will keep young people from participating outside "gender appropriate roles" (Griffin and Genasci, 1990; Rotella and Murray, 1991). Secondly, peer groups, parents and friends may discourage young people from participating in some sports or teams because of homosexual stigmas attached to that sport or team (Griffin, 1993b; Bennett et al., 1989).

The link between homophobia and women's sport appears to stem from the ideology that sport was a masculine preserve

---

[1] This Olympics had the highest ever number of women participants; however, male participants still outnumbered females by a ratio of 2 to 1.

because it was aggressive, physical and competitive. This is a view that is expressed by many writers. Pronger, for example, describes sport as a social arena where "athletics as a masculine drama involves the display of power, aggression and violence" (1994, p. 187). Hargreaves (1994), in discussing the early years of women's sport and physical education, claims that there were three charges put forth by critics against women's involvement in sport. Firstly, it was believed that too much exercise would damage the female reproductive capacity. Secondly, there was the notion that the excitement of sport would cause women to lose control. Thirdly, there was the fear that female athletes would adopt masculine styles of dress, talk, haircuts and mannerisms. An early impact from these views is that, in 1933, the Athletic Federation of College Women's Conference minimised team sports and advocated activities such as tennis, golf and horse riding as "life time sports with carry over value" (cited in Cahn, 1994, p. 49).

Homophobia as a Form of Social Control

A common theme that emerges amongst writers on the theme of homophobia and sport is that sport serves several functions in maintaining the traditional gender roles of both men and women. Griffin (1993b) discussed the presence of women in sport where they were competitive, skilful and aggressive. In these instances, she claimed that their physically strong presence appeared to threaten the special status of sport for men. Lenskyj (1990) argues that one hegemonic response has been that the entry of women into sport has been controlled. The control measures include the portrayal of participation by women in sport as un-feminine and belittling women's participation in sport and physical activity. An insight into how these views may impact on women's participation can be gleamed from the following incident which happened in 1998.

Ladies Gaelic Football is one of the fastest-growing women's sports in Ireland but does not have the support of one local County Councillor, who went on local radio after unsuccessfully opposing a €1,200 VEC grant for the promotion of ladies football. He said that "girls are too precious for such pursuits and sports fanatic fathers without sons are pushing their daughters to play these games". He further asserted that "a girl's body is too precious to be abused, bumped and humped playing football . . . they have their own natural humps and bumps which should not be abused by playing soccer and football" (quoted in article by Eugene Hogan, the *Irish Independent*, October 1998). Whilst these views are extreme, they received national coverage and sent shock waves amongst female Gaelic football players and sports enthusiasts in general. They also give an indication of the types of barriers that women still face in playing what were once traditionally considered to be male sports.

Whilst Bennett et al. (1989) note that significant progress has been made in the 1970s and 1980s, they claim that performances by women in sport are still stigmatised, marginalised and trivialised. They, along with Griffin (1993b) and Lenskyj (1990), argue that the most effective method of discouraging female participation in sport is to question the sexual orientation of female athletes, i.e. to assume that women who participate in certain sports are lesbians. In this way, homophobia operates as a form of social control. This prevents women's full participation in sport and often discredits and degrades them through accusations about their sexual orientation.

According to Griffin, "sexism and homophobia combine to marginalise and intimidate women by imposing societal expectations of what is acceptable sports participation for women" (1993b, p. 193). According to Bennett et al. (1989), these control measures are manifested in a number of ways that directly impact on women's participation in sport:

- Girls have restricted access to the sports experience and are often discouraged from taking part in certain sports;

- By being channelled away from sport, girls are growing up with minimal movement skills and are therefore likely to be less competent at sports activities and consequently less likely to take up or remain active in sport;

- Because some female athletes are suspect, they are less likely to be offered commercial contracts and sponsorship deals. As a result, the female adolescent is less likely to have a female sporting role model.

The above factors may particularly constrain teenage girls as their concern with their body image is closely associated with their increasing awareness of their sexual identity. Griffin (1993) in particular outlines the eagerness with which most adolescent girls pursue the establishment of their heterosexual identity. This may be exacerbated by added pressure from their peer group to conform. Cockerill and Hardy claim that:

> As the female teenager appears to place great emphasis on catching and retaining a "proper boyfriend", any factor, including enthusiastic participation in PE lessons and extra-curricular teams and clubs, which lead to a perceived loss of femininity will be avoided by those girls that regard this as a major objective (1987, p. 9).

What would appear clear is that, within a female adolescent subculture that is dominated by traditional ideas of femininity and heterosexual partnerships, a perceived association with lesbianism could represent a fundamental contradiction to the core values and expectations of many girls.

PERPETUATION OF TRADITIONAL STEREOTYPES

Hargreaves (1994), in discussing the influence of peer groups on female adolescent leisure behaviour, felt that images portrayed by the mass media had a strong influence in perpetuating the stereotypical conception of femininity. She goes on to suggest that women's use of time seems to be almost exclusively portrayed as a function of the needs of their families. This function of women as *servicing* family leisure is frequently portrayed in television advertisements. Common examples of this include advertising on the national media of mothers washing their sons' football kits.

Incantalupo (1994) expands on this theme in studying the portrayal of women in sports advertising. Two women's fitness magazines, *Women's Sports and Fitness* and *Shape*, were examined over the period 1985–90. They were compared during these years to determine changes within each magazine in the five-year period and also to compare differences between the magazines during the same period. This research established that there was an improvement in both magazines in their portrayal of the sporting women as being physically active. However, there was a difference between the magazines in their overall portrayal of women. Women appearing in advertisements in *Shape* magazine were less often shown actively participating. Frequently, they were depicted in situations where there were sexual overtones. Similarly, they were more often portrayed with isolated body parts and more likely to be depicted in swimsuits but not near water, than women appearing in *Women's Sport and Fitness*. According to Incantalupo (1994), *Shape* magazine appeared to be more interested in portraying women as sexual rather than as sporting beings.

Messner (1988) and McPherson et al. (1989) both discuss the differential treatment of women's sport in the mass media. There are several clear patterns which emerge:

- When women are featured in the media, much of the coverage is allocated to sports that confirm a feminine image of sport (tennis, ice-skating, gymnastics) or trivialise women's sports;

- There is little coverage of women's team sports;

- Women featured are often cast in a negative light such as flawed heroines, emotionally troubled, lonely, torn by conflict and as being unusual people.

There are many examples to illustrate the above points. For example, at the Atlanta Olympics in 1996, women were shown competing most often in two sports, namely gymnastics and diving. This was to such an extent that an exhibition by the winning gymnasts was broadcast by NBC whilst whole track events were not shown. The lack of screening of women's team sports on Irish national television has been a hotly contested point in recent years in Ireland. In the Irish national basketball finals each year, the men's final is shown live and only highlights are shown of the women's final on RTE. Similarly, in 1996, RTE caused controversy by failing to show highlights of the Women's Gaelic Football All-Ireland Final until the following Saturday. This was despite the fact that there were over 10,000 people at the game.

The men's final was shown live and replayed again on the same evening of the game. Even the minor game was shown live.

When Michael Carruth won a gold medal for boxing at the Olympic Games in Barcelona in 1992, he received considerable acclaim in the national media. When Sonia O'Sullivan won a gold medal for the 5,000 metres at the subsequent Athletics World Championships, there was considerable controversy. Much attention was focused on the fact that she had failed to don an Irish Tricolour for her victory lap. Many viewers and reviewers claimed she was unpatriotic. When Michelle Smith won three gold and a bronze medal at the Atlanta Olympics, there was considerably controversy in relation to her and performance-enhancing drugs. This is despite the fact that at this stage in her career she had never tested positive for banned substances. For many, she was a flawed heroine.

It is not only the media that helps perpetuate the stereotyping of female sports participation. Diller and Houston (1983) and Lynch (1989) refer to the hidden curriculum for girls' physical learning. The hidden curriculum runs counter to the explicit values and directives for physical education and means that girls learn to accept gender-differentiated constraints on their physical movements, while male-imposed limits on their rights to physical space are established and maintained by physical intimidation. They also maintain that the girls' physical space is circumscribed and confined in direct contrast to the physical freedom given to boys. Girls also learn that their games are devalued while the one and only physical priority for their own sex is physical beauty.

Hargreaves (1994) has documented that throughout history, women have been told that vigorous exercise, sweating, muscular development and serious competition, particularly when this is against men, is un-feminine. The consequence of this perpetuation of stereotypical images of women's sport, whether it is by the mass media, the educational system or society at large, is that the female athlete is either discouraged, ignored or depicted in a less than ideal light, resulting in there being few positive female sporting role models for young girls. Thus, they may be less likely to actively participate in sport or physical activity.

SOCIALISATION

McPherson et al. (1989) define socialisation as the

> complex developmental learning process that teaches the knowledge, values and norms essential to participation in social life . . . through socialisation we learn all types of social roles — sex roles, work roles, leisure roles — and develop a sense of self (p. 37).

The primary agency of socialisation is the family, and Greendorfer (1983) was of the view that other social institutions such as the school, peer groups and the mass media "merely reinforce what has been initiated in the family. This is especially true when it comes to beliefs and behaviour in sport" (p. 26). Greendorfer has been one of the pioneers in researching sports socialisation in childhood sport. She came to the conclusion that

> instead of challenging the pervasive viewpoint that low female participation in sport is part of the natural order, low rates of participation are the result of a chain of events which begins during early infancy and has life long consequences (p. 24).

In the early years, the socialisation of children's behaviour takes a number of forms. Almost from birth, baby girls are more frequently touched, handled and talked to than baby boys (Byrne, 1978; Howarth, 1988). On the other hand, boys are more often allowed to explore their environment without intervention from their parents whilst girls are treated protectively and restrained (Greendorfer, 1983). This differential treatment appears to contribute to girls becoming less independent in their behaviour than boys. Parents continue to be more protective of girls as they grow up. Thus, girls are more often encouraged into scheduled leisure activities while boys are not as constrained in the activities they can engage in (Smoll, 1996; Hendry et al., 1993).

From an early age, gender stereotyping often becomes quite marked. Boys and girls receive toys and games perceived by parents and relatives to be appropriate to their biological gender. Girls would therefore often get presents of dolls and boys footballs. According to McPherson et al. (1989), such practices tend to continue through childhood to the extent that "sport is more likely to become part of the value system and social repertoire of males" (p. 40). Behaviourally, there are gender differences that are encouraged by parents. Greendorfer (1983) found that girls were encouraged to behave like *good* girls and to play quietly and are discouraged from taking part in activities which are excessively rough, active or noisy, and as a result "habits and values towards inactivity become incorporated into the lifestyles of most females" (p. 16). Girls are therefore not socialised into sports to the same extent as boys. When the participation rates are tracked into adolescence, the differences in participation levels, particularly for competitive sports, are clear (Mason, 1995; Kremer et al., 1997; Hendry et al., 1993). While there has been a marked improvement in the participation rates in sports by girls, the differences are still significant. Figure 4.1 below shows that while there were significant improvements in the participation rates of girls relative to boys in the 1970s in US high schools, the significant differences have remained remarkably constant since then.

Figure 4.1: Number of Boys and Girls Participating in Interscholastic Athletics in US, 1972 to 1992

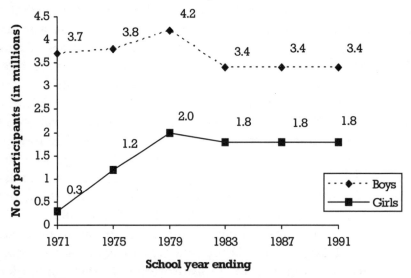

Source: National Federation of State High Schools Associations (1993).

Chapter 5

THE CONCEPT OF ADOLESCENCE AND TRENDS IN LEISURE AND LIFESTYLE PATTERNS AMONGST ADOLESCENTS

This chapter explores the notion of adolescence and looks at some of the current leisure and lifestyle patterns of adolescents as outlined in the available literature. The literature suggests that societal changes are blurring the distinction between adolescence and adulthood. The second half of the chapter focuses on some of the changing trends in leisure and lifestyle patterns, and in particular the impact of information and communication technologies.

ADOLESCENCE

The concept of adolescence is relatively new and is in many ways a product of the twentieth century. Up until then, adulthood was imposed on children from an early age. This was mainly the result of economic necessity. Giddens (1994) relates that it was common for children to be sent to work from as young as seven years of age. This is still the case in many parts of the world. Moleres (1998) claimed that Brazil has seven million workers under the age of seventeen, one in six Filipino children work and that a child can contribute 25 per cent of a family's income in India. This issue of children working has been tackled by a recent UN convention which urged governments not merely to ban underage labour, which would push families further into poverty, but to improve working conditions and reduce hours to make time for schooling. In the developed world, adolescence has distinct connotations. Hendry et al. describe adolescence

> as a time for waiting, developing and maturing and for accomplishing the rites of passage between childhood and adult status, it is certainly an extended phase of life for today's young people (1993, p. 1).

Philosophers such as Jean Jacques Rousseau and John Locke were early writers who promoted the notion of a separateness of childhood from adulthood. Their writings in the seventeenth and eighteenth centuries first brought an awareness of children as separate individuals with different needs and capacities to adults. Neil Postman (1985) suggests that it was the advent of the printing press that led to the development of the idea of childhood. The need for literacy was a natural divider between child and adult. The invention of printing combined with the forces of industrialisation introduced a perceived need for mass education. Children were sent to school until they became adults. School became the world of childhood, thus reinforcing the idea even further, especially among the bourgeois class. Aries claims that adults thus controlled both what the schoolchild was taught and also the rate of learning by children:

> . . . this led to a remarkable change in the social status of the young. Because the school was designed for preparation of the literate adult, the young came to be seen not as miniature adults but as something quite different altogether — uninformed adults. School learning became identified with the special nature of childhood . . . childhood became defined by school attendance (1960, p. 55).

Adults thus had the opportunity for unprecedented social control over children and to control both the learning environment and also what they were allowed to learn

> to a considerable extent, developments were dictated by the nature of both books and school. By writing sequenced textbooks and by organising school classes according to calendar age, schoolmasters invented, as it were, the stages of childhood (Postman, 1985, p. 45).

However, a number of writers have argued vehemently against the increasing influential role of school on the child within society. The social critic Ivan Illich, in his classic treatise *Deschooling Society*, argues against compulsory schooling not on the grounds that schools were un-improvable but even more so, that compulsory schooling effectively bars the young from fully participating in the life of the community and actually prevents them from becoming adults.

ADOLESCENCE AS A PERIOD OF TRANSITION

There are a number of classical theories that have established certain views about adolescence and are reflected in modern views about the transition from childhood to adolescence. Early work by Mead in primitive societies brought to public attention the differing effects of cultural forces on young people's development. The "Storm and Stress"[1] analogy espoused by Stanley Hall is still influential, as is Freud's idea that human behaviour is motivated by psycho-sexual forces. Davis's (1990) book *Youth and the Condition of Britain: Images of Adolescent Conflict* traces, in a historical context, many of the public images of adolescents in society. Some of the recurring themes explored are the themes of rebellion, angst, delinquency, energy, excitement and idealistic views of future society. Jones (1988) maintains that it was not until the 1950s that adolescents became truly visible in Britain. He linked this development to the post-war Education Act. Coleman (1961) identified a similar trend in the US around the same period. He described the school as taking over the natural processes of education in the family and setting the adolescent apart from the rest of society.

There is now an academic preference among writers to view adolescence as a transitional process rather than as a stage or a series of stages (Hendry, et al. 1993; Davis, 1990; Coleman et al., 1990). There are a number of factors that affect the rate of development of the individual adolescent. Internal factors to the adolescent would include physiological and emotional pres-

---

[1] This refers to the frequent tantrums as well as the stressful periods which are often cited as a feature of adolescence.

sure. The adolescent is also subjected to external pressures that include parents, teachers, their peers and greater society in general. Hendry et al. (1993) maintain that there are two main classical explanations within the transition process of adolescence. The first is the psychoanalytic approach that concentrates on the psychosexual factors that underlie the young person's move away from childhood behaviour and emotional involvement. The second is sociological or social-psychological. This sees the causes of transition in adolescence as lying primarily in the social setting and concentrates on the nature of roles and role conflict and the relative influence of significant others.

Coleman (1979) attempted to bridge these clearly interdependent analytical approaches when he developed his focal theory model as illustrated in Figure 5.1 below.

Figure 5.1: Coleman's Focal Issues Model

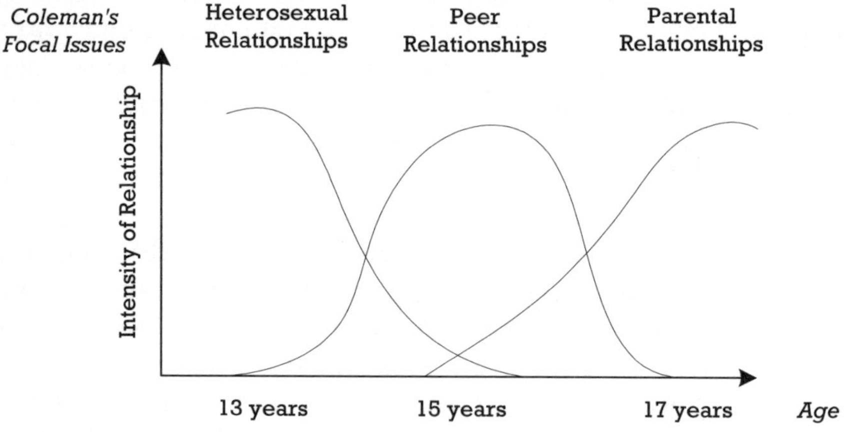

Source: J.S. Coleman, 1979

In this theory, Coleman suggests that gender roles and relationships with the opposite sex declines from a peak at the age of about thirteen years. Their concerns about acceptance by or rejection from peers is significant around fifteen years while issues regarding the gaining of independence from parents climb steadily to peak around the age of sixteen years and then tail off.

Hendry et al. (1993) applied this theory to leisure participation and found transitions that matched the relational issues suggested by Coleman. In a longitudinal study of 10,000 Scottish teenagers, Hendry et al. found that the leisure focus through the adolescent years initially shows a strong reliance by the young adolescent on adult-organised clubs and activities. The next phase of their leisure development shows a move towards casual leisure pursuits and the final stage is a leaning towards commercially organised leisure.

THE FADING DISTINCTION BETWEEN ADOLESCENCE AND ADULTHOOD

Postman (1985) puts forward the argument that there is a fading distinction between adolescence and adulthood. He argues this view from a number of angles which will now be discussed.

Merging Tastes and Styles of Adolescents and Adults

Popular adolescent fashions have become more adult-like. Similarly, junk food is as popular with adults as adolescents. The same trend carries over to entertainment. The Nielsen reports on programmes watched on television in America revealed a remarkable similarity between the favourite shows of adolescents and adults. There has been a similar merging of taste between adult and youthful taste in music. Postman's theory could well be projected forward to this new millennium. A particularly good example would be the recent trend of junior certificate going on holidays to Ibiza just like their adult counterparts.

Changing Perspectives of Social Institutions such as the Law, the Schools and Sport

There has been in recent years a consistent move towards children's rights. A number of high profile court cases have demonstrated the extent to which society now values the rights of children. In 1995, a Florida teenager successfully divorced himself from his parents. A British twelve-year-old took his stepfather to the European Court in 1996 to legally prevent him being slapped. In the Irish courts, children can now be taken from their parents in certain circumstances and be made wards of the courts. Another landmark case in 1997, which is referred to as in the "C" case, concerned a thirteen-year-old girl who was raped. She was allowed have an abortion in England despite the fact that her parents wanted her to have the child. In Sweden, as in many other countries, it is now illegal for parents to slap their children, while in Ireland corporal punishment has been banned in schools since the early 1970s. The key importance of children's rights is exemplified in article 3 of the UNICEF *Convention on the Rights of the Child* which states:

> In all actions concerning children, whether undertaken by public or private social welfare institutions, courts of law, administrative authorities or legislative bodies, the best interests of the child shall be a primary consideration (1996, p. 3).

Similarly in schools, adolescents have been granted increasing access to any information that is held about them. They now have the right to appeal against results gained in national exams and have been increasingly making use of this facility. They also have rights in relation to attendance or non-attendance at religious instruction classes and, in general, they are gaining increasing rights in many spheres of their lives.

In sports, too, there is evidence of the merging of adolescent and adult values. Andrews and O'Connor (1990) have noted a decline in unsupervised street games. However, it is the increasing professionalisation, the seriousness and the organisation of youth sport which have witnessed the greatest changes. Many parents and teachers are now party to a system where children play their games under careful supervision and without spontaneity. The banning of running in the schoolyard during playtime by many schools would reflect this trend.[2] Children's play has become an adult preoccupation and it is no longer separate from the world of adults. This is probably best illustrated by the furore in the national media when there was a free-for-all fight amongst parents at an under-ten Gaelic football league game in County Wicklow in 1997. In the resulting

---

[2] Although teachers blame insurance requirements for this rule, it does appear to reflect a general trend away from spontaneous play.

skirmish, the referee was also attacked in what should have been a game of little significance to be enjoyed by the children involved. The motivation by parents to develop the sporting abilities of their children has led in some cases to the entry of children into competing at the highest level in a number of sports. A classic example of this phenomenon is Tiger Woods, who was introduced to golf at three years of age by his father and given intensive coaching in early primary school. Another good example is the case of the Williams sisters in tennis.

In some sports, this practice has been acceptable for many years. Young gymnasts, divers and swimmers have dominated international competitions for several years now. Even in sports like tennis, there have been child prodigies. At a grand slam women's event in 1997, which was won by Martina Hingis who was then sixteen, her opponent was just one year older. The most obvious answer to this phenomenon is that better coaching and training techniques have made it possible for children to attain or even surpass adult competence levels. Postman (1985) argues that the traditional arguments about the uniqueness of children are disappearing. The idea of play for play's sake is fast fading and, increasingly, play is linked with some external purpose, such as renown, money, physical conditioning, upward mobility or national pride. For adults, play is serious business. In Postman's view, as childhood disappears, so too does the child's view of play.

Evidence from Statistical Figures concerning Crime, Alcohol Usage, Drug Use and Sexual Activity

There are a number of key statistical facts that also appear to indicate the merging of behaviour of adolescents and adults. One such example is crime. In America, for example, the number of serious crimes[3] committed by juveniles as a proportion of the total crime committed has been consistently growing since the 1950s, as shown in Table 5.1 below.[4]

---

[3] Defined by the FBI to include crimes such as murder, forcible rape, robbery and aggravated assault.

[4] Defined in American law as under fifteen years.

Table 5.1: Likelihood of an Over-fifteen-year-old Committing Crime as Opposed to an Under-fifteen-year-old

1950	215 times more likely
1960	8 times more likely
1980	5.5 time more likely

Source: Postman, 1985, p. 131.

This figure is even greater when taken with the fact that the overall rate of crime is on the increase. Therefore, the rate of juvenile crime is increasing at a significantly faster rate than adult crime. These trends are reflected in Irish cities and towns. Juvenile crime increased by 10 per cent in Waterford City in 1997 (Hogan, 1998). The local juvenile liaison officer linked the rise in crime to the prevalence of drugs and especially alcohol abuse. Interestingly, he stated that

> many parents are so terrified of their children getting in-
> volved with drugs that they seem to be blind to the damage
> that alcohol causes (p. 1).

Many adolescents are engaging in the adult activities of drinking and smoking and the numbers involved have been well-documented (Grube, Joel and Morgan, 1986, 1990, 1994; Doorly and Hynes, 1995; Dept. of Health, 1999). In 1993, the Health Promotion Unit of the Department of Health commissioned a study to examine smoking and drinking among young people. A representative sample of 4,000 students between the ages of twelve and eighteen in 80 second-level schools were questioned about smoking and drinking. Of these, a total of 57 per cent of males and 53 per cent of females had tried smoking. These figures came down to 17 per cent of males and 15 per cent of females for those who smoked on a daily basis. The peak ages for smoking were sixteen and seventeen.

Whilst the figures for smoking would appear to be high, the figures for drinking show that even higher numbers of adolescents have tried drinking. A total of 63 per cent have taken an alcoholic drink. This includes a figure of 41 per cent at thirteen years of age or younger. Male and female figures are similar, particularly in the later school years. The only major difference is that a higher percentage of boys appear to start drinking at the earlier age of thirteen to fourteen years. The numbers who claim to be regular drinkers are almost a third for boys (32 per cent) and for girls just over a quarter (27 per cent). Thus, almost three out of every ten school-going teenagers in this study claimed to be regular drinkers. Societal attitudes to selling drink and cigarettes appear to be liberal in Ireland. Only 10 per cent had ever been refused cigarettes even though it is illegal to buy cigarettes if you are under sixteen. The proportion refused alcohol was in the region of 20 per cent even though it is illegal for those under eighteen to buy drink. It would appear that those adolescents who are drinking or smoking have little difficulty sourcing their cigarettes or drinks.

The level of addiction to both alcohol and drugs amongst a percentage of adolescents is an area that many youth workers and politicians have urged the government to tackle for several years. Fr Joe Young, a priest who works with the community in Southhill, a strongly working-class area in Limerick, is the addiction counsellor for his diocese. He has consistently stated that there is an urgent need for an addiction centre for teenagers in Ireland. There is currently no dedicated centre for adolescents. This on-the-ground feeling is confirmed by a survey, funded by the Department of Health (1999), which was carried out by Dr Mark Moran, a psychologist at St Patrick's College, Dublin. In a survey of 50,000 sixteen-year-olds across 26 European countries, Ireland had the highest percentage of binge drinkers. A figure of 23 per cent reported binge drinking (three times or more in the month before the survey). Furthermore, 87 per cent of the Irish sixteen-year-olds claimed to have taken a drink in the previous year and a figure of 66 per cent claimed to have been drunk in the previous year.

Another key area in which adolescents have appeared to emulate adults is the area of sexual activity. The most tangible evidence of this is in the increase in the recorded number of teenage pregnancies each year. It would appear that Postman's view in relation to the fading distinction between childhood and adulthood would be supported by the above trends.

KEY SOCIAL CHANGES IN YOUTHS

In recent years, many traditional values, norms and social relations are either being changed or questioned. The traditional image of youth is also changing. Some of the key social changes are outlined below:

- Adolescents are remaining in education longer and there is a noticeable delay in entering the workforce. This is best exemplified by the legal school-leaving age, which has reflected this phenomenon in Ireland: 1972 — raised to fifteen years; 1999 — raised to sixteen years.

- The Irish government is keen to keep Irish youths in the education system. In fact it was a stated aim of the government to have a 90 per cent retention rate in senior cycle education by the year 2000 (DES, 1995).

- Whilst youth in the past was a period of transition, in recent times it has been marketed as a phase of its own. There are specific magazines, musical bands and branded goods that are aimed specifically at the adolescent market.

- The clear separation between childhood and adulthood is becoming more diffuse. Sexual activity and drinking, for example, which were considered adult activities, appear to be widely practised by many adolescents.

- Children's rights have improved and the authoritarian system of control would appear to be fading. It is no longer the norm for parents to proscribe rules. It is more likely that rules and behaviour of teenagers will be to some extent negotiated.

- The notion of the competent adult is fading. This has come about primarily as a result of technology. As adolescents are often more competent in the use of technology than their parents, this has reduced the importance of parents as socialising agents.

TELEVISION VIEWING BY ADOLESCENTS

There has been little research to date on the socialisation effect of television on adolescents in Ireland. However, what does appear clear from other available research is that watching television is the predominant leisure pastime of many adolescents. Some of the available data confirm the widespread practice of television viewing. In the UK, there is a television in 98 per cent of all homes (Gunter and McAleer, 1997). Research by Nielsen Media Research (cited in Strasburger, 1995) in the US also found an identical figure of 98 per cent of homes having at least one television. Interestingly, it was found that more homes in the US had televisions than had indoor plumbing, which gives an indication that the television is now viewed as more of a basic necessity in houses than some of the more traditional utilities. Whilst 98 per cent of the population had one television set in the US, 66 per cent of households had two or more televisions. Similarly in the UK, it appears to be becoming the norm to have two or more televisions, particularly when there are children in the house.

An important issue that will affect the available time for sporting activities is how much television adolescents watch. Nielsen Media Research found that the average teenager watched 22 hours of television per week. These data included network and cable viewing but did not include movies viewed on a videocassette recorder (VCR) or the use of video or computer games. When VCR and video games were added to the equation, the average teenager spent between 35 and 55 hours a week in front of a television set. These figures are higher than the British figures. The Broadcasters' Audience Research Board (BARB) publishes the official viewing figures in the United Kingdom. The figures for daily viewing when analysed longitudinally show a trend to increased consumption of the television medium by teenagers, as seen in Table 5.2 below.

Table 5.2: Number of Hours Spent Watching Television Each Day by Teenagers

Year	12–15-year olds	16–24-year-olds
1983	2.1	2.2
1984	2.6	2.2
1992	2.6	2.5
1993	2.8	2.8
1994	2.7	2.8

Source: BARB 1983–1995, cited in Gunter and McAleer (1997, p. 6).

Strasburger (1995) puts the data into context when he compares the number of hours spent watching television against the number of hours spent in school (up to the end of high school) in the US. He computes that the average teenager will by this stage have spent 15,000–18,000 hours in front of a television set as opposed to 12,000 hours in the classroom. Most young people would therefore appear to spend more time watching television than any other activity except sleeping.

There is thus a strong argument that television displaces traditional leisure activities. Many educationalists have expressed concern about the effect of television on activities such as reading. The same query can be postulated in relation to sports participation. Does the amount of time spent watching television leave sufficient time for sports participation? The situation is exacerbated by the increasing availability of other information and communication technologies (ICT).[5] There is now a wide and increasing array of ICT including such accessories as video recorders, remote controls, personal computers and game consoles. The Department of Education and Science is also aiming to train all Irish school children in the use of ICT. In fact, all Irish primary and second-level schools were connected to the Internet in 1998. As far back as 1986, a UK nationwide study of 486 young people aged between four and twelve years showed that:

---

[5] Particularly computer usage as part of their IT 2000 project.

- 96 per cent had a computer in their school

- 93 per cent had a cassette for listening to music tapes

- 83 per cent had a record player

- 70 per cent had a musical instrument to play

- 65 per cent had their own radio

- 52 per cent had a VCR in their home

- 43 per cent had their own television set.

Source: A study by Gunter and Greenberg, 1986, published in the *Times Education Supplement*, October 1986.

Larson examined where teenagers watched television. The bedroom emerged as a most significant location for teens. Larson asserted that it was here that they engaged in solitary media use to "cultivate a newly discovered self". He further asserted that while television was used to disengage, music was used to "directly engage with issues of identity" (1995, p. 536). Another recent lifestyle trend that is being engaged in by an increasing number of adolescents is the use of mobile phones. About four million British children are believed to have mobile phones. While one in three adults in the UK has a mobile phone, the percentage of under-eighteens that uses them has risen from 15 per cent in 1998 to 35 per cent in 1999 and to 70 per cent in 2002.

Research by one of the service providers gives some interesting findings. It suggests that children follow the same behavioural pattern. For the first month, under adult supervision, they use their phones for less than five minutes a day, after which it shoots up to 40 minutes, while a fifth use their phones for more than two hours a day. Most of these high-end users are teenage girls aged between thirteen and sixteen.[6] The use of the mobile phone would therefore appear to be another competitor for the adolescent's time, particularly amongst girls.

The media may play a significant role in gender role socialisation. Bandura (1994) in promoting the social learning theory

---

[6] Figures quoted in an article by John Harlow in the *Sunday Times*, September 1999.

argued that children learn behaviour by observing others in real life and vicariously through the media. A 1988 report by Steenland examined how adolescent girls were displayed in 200 episodes of programming. She found that:

- Teenage girls' looks are portrayed as being more important than their brains;

- Intelligent girls are sometimes portrayed as being social misfits;

- Teenage girls are more passive than their male counterparts;

- TV frequently shows girls as being obsessed with shopping, grooming and dating;

- 94 per cent of teenage girls on TV are middle class or wealthy.

It would appear that ICT has been playing a significant and increasing part in the life of teenagers now for some time. With the increasing availability and reducing cost of technology, it appears that sport faces considerable competition for time with the existing and new technologies in the coming years.

Chapter 6

CHANGING TRENDS IN YOUTH SPORT

There has been a consistent increase in both sports participation and the awareness of sport as displayed by young people right across Europe. Crum (1991) labels this the "sportification of society" (p. 15). However, the nature of sport itself has been influenced by societal changes. A number of sports models now exist. As well as the evolution of elite and top-level sports, there has been the parallel growth in the alternative sports experience with immediate gratification, recreation and relaxation as the main characteristics of these forms of sport. These have led to the development of new and varied forms of sport such as leisure sports like indoor soccer; adventure sports like bungee jumping; and health activities like pilates or aerobics. Crum (1991) refers to this as the "desportification of society" (p. 17) while Dietrich and Heinemann (1989) refer to these alternate sport forms as "non-sporting sport" (p. 43). These two evolutions concerning the identity and role of sport within society have been brought about by a number of societal changes in recent years. These changes and the worldwide trends in youth sport will be discussed in this chapter.

DEMOGRAPHIC TRENDS

Demographic trends have and do influence sports participation trends. The available data from Eurostat (1992) predict that in the next 30 years, fewer children will be born within the European Union. The net result is that predictions estimate 16.8 million fewer youngsters (up to age nineteen) in 2020 than in 1990. Certain sections in Ireland are acutely aware of this trend which will impact heavily on this country. The second-level population has peaked, meaning there will be significantly fewer students in the coming years. There will thus be fewer adolescents available to field sports teams. The corresponding ageing of the population is likely to lead to pressure groups forming to promote the case for masters' sport which may result in less interest and money for youth sport (Clearing House, 1988). The stark reality of the declining numbers is a worry for many sporting bodies. In an article in *The Sunday Times* (August 1999), the PRO of the Offaly GAA county board summed up the harsh reality facing his county:

> In 1980, over 1,500 babies were born in Offaly. In 1994, that figure was 750. Say about half of them were boys, that's a very small number to pick a team from in 2011 — a minor (under-18) hurling team and a minor football team.

PARTICIPATION TRENDS

It is clear from the available research that the general popularity of sport is increasing. This is particularly the case with organised sports participation (Clearing House, 1988; Ban, 1990; De Knop et al., 1991). However, there have been significant changes in the types and structure of activities that are now being participated in by adolescents. For instance, several studies have shown that after the age of fourteen, there is a clear and dramatic drop-off in membership in sports clubs (Campbell, 1988; Seppanean, 1982; Stensaasen, 1982). So although youth sport is a fast-developing area, it is not attracting all young people. There is also the added problem of the high drop-out from sport by adolescents. As a result, Mulligan (1999) claims that it is critical that adolescents are introduced to a large variety of sports and that certain sports need to be adapted to attract the interest of adolescents.

Individualisation is another trend that is impacting sharply on sport. Beckers (1989) and Roberts and Kamphorst (1990) have highlighted this cultural trend and its impact on sport. There is a decreasing influence by family, neighbourhood and church and political organisations on the adolescent's behaviour and sports preferences. As a result, leisure activities among youths have become more informal. The British Sports Council had identified such a trend as particularly problematic for team sports as far back as 1982. By implication, therefore, the playing of national team games in Ireland would appear to be under threat. The GAA, in particular, prides itself on its extensive links with families, schools, the church and especially the club unit. Whilst this sporting organisation in Ireland has been reluctant to admit that there are problem areas, a survey of hurling among 3,185 students in Wexford schools in 1995 clearly showed a decline in youth interest in this sport within their county. Another trend which is closely identified with individualisation is commonly referred to as "cocooning" (Dietrich and Heinemann, 1989, p. 11). This refers to the growing popularity of practising sport within the private sphere of home. This would also appear to be a factor of affluence and the availability of money to purchase, for example, home gyms or the space to have a table-tennis table, a tennis court or a basketball hoop. Thus, there is increasing competition to get the adolescent away from home for physical activities such as team games. Adolescents also have the increasingly attractive option of home-based passive leisure activities such as home computers, televisions and other ICT.

THE COMMERCIALISATION OF SPORT

Since the 1980s, there has been an increasing commercialisation, professionalisation and privatisation within the sports domain. This has been led in many instances by changing government policy that is probably best reflected by Thatcherite policy in the UK. Policies such as the introduction of compulsory, competitive tendering have particularly changed the nature of public leisure provision in the UK. De Knop et al. (1996) claim that there has been a shift from the provision of collective facilities to an increasing emphasis on private initiatives.

Sport is now a branded product and the increasing commercialisation within sport is evident. Consumers can choose from an increasing number of programmes, events and facilities from the cultural, sporting and tourist domains. Sky now have three television channels devoted exclusively to sports whilst newspapers and several magazines devote sections to

sport. Many sports are now operating in differing circumstances than even five to ten years ago. Quite apart from other
sports, there is also the increasing competition from alternative
leisure activities. Probably more significant is the influence of
BSkyB. Because of the sheer exposure that Sky gives to sports
this has placed many sports organisations in a dilemma. The
Football Association in England has embraced Sky to their advantage. A significant bastion within the Rugby Union tried to
maintain their independence and amateur ethos but economic
requirements have meant that changes have occurred in their
sport to accommodate television programming requirements.

The GAA in Ireland prides itself on being an autonomous
organisation and would support relationships with terrestrial
Irish television channels. However, they have not ruled out a
relationship with Sky in the future. Their Chief Executive Officer
said, in relation to Sky involvement, "never say never".[1] However, national sporting bodies have also reacted in subtle ways
to this pressure. In adapting to these trends, many sports organisations have introduced alternate and/or complementary
forms to their sports disciplines. The growth of the mini-sport
movement in practically all the major sports, indoor rock climb-
ing and indoor hurling are all examples of this trend.

The process of commercialisation has turned sport into big
business. One result of this is that the economic value has su-
perseded some of the traditional values of sport. Sewart (1987)
refers to the "commodification of sport" (p. 171). At one extreme, i.e. the elite level, this has led to the destruction of the
idealised model of sport with its traditional ritualistic meaning.
The use of anabolic steroids, transfer bungs by soccer manag-
ers, match fixing and institutionalised cheating are examples of
the changing nature of sport. Sewart asserts that the commodification of sport is evidenced in three arenas:

- Changes in rules, format and scheduling

- The abandonment of the ethic of skill democracy

---

[1] Quote from Liam Mulvihill, cited in the *Irish Independent* from the 1996
Easter GAA congress.

- The move towards spectacle and theatricality.

There are many examples where rules have been changed to make the sport more of a spectacle. For instance, the Rugby Union has increased the points for a try from three to four to five points over the years to encourage more try scoring, which is the most exciting aspect of the game for spectators. Rule changes have been introduced in volleyball and tennis to make it easier to schedule television advertising. The format of American football has also been altered to accommodate television advertisements. The scheduling of sports events has led to several controversies in recent years. This particularly applies to world games where different time zones mean that sports may be scheduled to suit the television viewing needs of different countries. In the World Cup in soccer in 1994, Ireland had to play Holland in Florida under the midday sun in the middle of the summer. The men's marathon in Atlanta in the 1996 Olympics was also to be scheduled during the midday sun and was only altered after considerable protests from athletes and warnings from medical personnel about the health risks of running such a gruelling event at that time.

Some sports have attempted to keep the skill level even amongst teams in a league. American football, for example, has its drafting procedure. The salary cap in the National Basketball Association is another example, whereby teams are not allowed to exceed certain agreed limits. However, in most sports, it is the bigger and wealthier clubs who can poach talented players from other clubs to maintain their dominance. The smaller clubs thus act in many ways as filters for the bigger clubs and are exploited by them. These trends are also impacting on adolescents. For example, in 1998 the Football Association of Ireland appointed a Career Guidance Officer. They did this because of several complaints of abuse and exploitation of young Irish soccer players in England.

The inclination to create a spectacle in sport is also increasing. For example, the All Ireland final in either hurling or football is no longer just a game between amateurs. There are now celebrations organised for several weeks around this game. On the day of the finals, there are singers and other side-show entertainments on offer. Similarly with the Olympics, the biggest attractions to the public are the opening and closing ceremonies. In Atlanta, tickets to the opening ceremonies cost upwards of $600 which is an indication of the demand for them. In the sports events themselves, moments of spectacle are constantly highlighted by the television cameras. The emotions of players and managers are shown in slow motion. Plays are shown from side angles, reverse angles and in slow motion. These plays are later analysed, often in minute detail.

The main purpose of this process is to attract more viewers and therefore make sport more commercially attractive. Sewart (1987) describes this process as

> instead of athletic contests which happen to be broadcast on television, the process of commodification has given television events which happen to include athletes (p. 178).

The process may mean that sports are marketed to be watched rather than played by adolescents.

However, it is not just in top-level sports that the commodification of sports has had an effect. The average sports participant has become increasingly demanding with regard to sports participation. Many older GAA players boast about changing for matches in the ditch. Nowadays, this would be unusual. The controversy of the threatened strike by the Cork hurlers in 2002 shows that even amateur players now demand not just the sports facilities and changing rooms but also the provision of infrastructural and supporting structures such as qualified coaches. This trend has profound implications for public sector leisure provision. For instance, in regard to swimming pool usage, research has indicated that a pool with recreational facilities will attract more visitors and be more profitable (Smeets, 1990). As a result, local authorities may be faced with the dilemma of renovating their facilities or closing them down.

Having examined these changing trends, their impact on the physical activity and leisure patterns of adolescents will now be examined. As there are so few studies that concentrate on adolescents, this section will concentrate on any Irish studies of physical activity patterns.

PHYSICAL ACTIVITY AND LEISURE TRENDS IN IRELAND

The general trend found in studies in Ireland to date show that a relatively low number of the population are committed to continuous involvement in physical activity. In a Health Education Bureau survey in 1984, O'Connor (1986) showed that 42 per cent of the population claimed to take some exercise. The majority of participants walked for exercise and there was a low percentage of women (13 per cent) who regularly participated in sports events.

O'Connor and Daly (1983) examined weekly participation rates of 942 West Limerick people. This study found a regular participation rate of 15 per cent. Foster (1984) did his study on 100 rural residents. He found a participation rate of 19 per cent and interestingly, he found a higher participation rate among females. This he partly attributed to the fact that many of the men were engaged in physical type work and therefore were not as keen to participate in activities such as walking. The figures were considerably higher in a study conducted by Noonan and O'Malley (1987). Their study was, however, concentrated on a follow-up study of 130 school leavers. They found that 62 per cent of females and 69 per cent of males regularly took part in recreational activities.

Drummy and Watson (1992) were commissioned by the Sports Research Council to carry out a study of the activity and lifestyle characteristics of Irish school children between the ages of ten and thirteen years. Their study followed on from two earlier studies that pointed to the need for further research. The first of these looked at the fitness levels of primary school children and found the average fitness level to be low (Watson, 1990a). A further study (Watson, 1990b), carried on this study into second-level schools and found that a quarter of all boys and a third of the girls were seriously lacking in aerobic fitness and half the males and a third of the girls had very inadequate levels of flexibility. These studies were in part motivated by an increasing public awareness and strong research findings, as Simons-Morton et al. (1988) point out:

not only because of its concurrent relationship with risk factors but also because of its possible influence on future adult
participation of physical activity (p. 405).

In their follow-up study, Drummy and Watson found that the activity levels of the Irish children were lower than their European
and American counterparts. For instance, a Dutch study in 1989
by Backx et al. reported that over 50 per cent of Dutch children
took part in six hours of activity or more per week. The Irish results were considerably lower than this mark. The results were
however just slightly lower than a comparable study in Northern Ireland.[2] Some interesting gender differences emerged in
this study. Boys, for example, enjoyed hard physical activity
whilst girls preferred light physical activity. It is not surprising
therefore that boys were thus found to be four times more likely
to be involved in hard physical activity than girls. Girls, on the
other hand, were significantly more diligent with their homework: 73 per cent of girls spent more than 90 minutes per night
on their homework as compared to 30 per cent of the boys.
Similarly, the girls had a better knowledge of diet and were
less likely to consume alcohol.

As many of these surveys were small and localised in their
nature, the Minister for Sport commissioned a major study in
1994 to establish national participation rates in sport. The aim of
this survey was to establish the percentage of Irish people between sixteen and 75 years of age who participated in sport and
physical activity and the level and intensity of their involvement. In March of that year, 2,000 door-to-door interviews were
carried out and a further 1,300 followed this in August to cover
the seasonal factors involved in participation.

The study showed considerably higher participation rates
than in previous Irish studies. The March study showed a participation rate in the previous week of 53 per cent, and this figure increased to 60 per cent for the August survey. This survey
would, however, appear to have been generous in assessing
what they meant by physical activity and this may explain the
discrepancy between activity levels as recorded in earlier

---

[2] The Northern Ireland Health and Fitness Study, 1989.

studies. For example, any type of walking was included as exercise, even if it was only a gentle stroll. Similarly, activities such as billiards and snooker were included, as were gardening and angling. Unfortunately, there are no available statistics on the female/male breakdown of these figures. However, figures on the reasons why people participate by gender are given in Table 6.1 below.

Table 6.1: Reasons for Participation (base: all who participate)

	Overall	Men	Women
To maintain good health	39%	35%	43%
To get outdoors/fresh air	36%	34%	38%
To make my life enjoyable	31%	36%	25%
For relaxation purposes	31%	31%	31%
To meet people/socialise	23%	25%	21%
To lose/maintain weight	20%	11%	29%
I enjoy the competition	15%	20%	9%
To occupy my spare time	13%	17%	9%
Because my friends/partner participate in it	12%	12%	13%
To release tension	11%	12%	10%

Source: "A National Survey of Involvement in Sport and Physical Activity", p. 28.

It is interesting to note the bias towards health reasons for women as their main reason for taking part in sport. Similarly, it is worth noting the higher percentage of men than women who are interested in competition.

Chapter 7

THE ROLE OF THE FAMILY

The term *familial aggregation* is used to categorise the combination of genetic and environmental influences within a family (Freedson and Evenson, 1991). The influence of parents is considered by many writers to be a critical determinant of whether or not children will be physically active (Sallis et al., 1992). Indeed, Dempsey et al. (1993) claim that the role of the family is *the* single most significant factor. The primal importance of parental influence on children's activity behaviour has instinctive appeal since parents have innumerable opportunities to influence the activity habits of their children. The arguments range here from parental inclusion of their children into their activities (Shropshire and Carroll, 1997), to the parents being enablers for their children. Parents may enable their children to participate by assisting in one or more of the following: they may act as coaches, may provide transport, may give encouragement, may provide money, may organise coaching or they may play with their children.

THE INFLUENCE OF THE FAMILY

Families can influence children's physical activities in many ways, with Brustad (1993b) emphasising the social, psychological and physical dimensions of adolescents' activity involvement. Perusse et al. (1989) outline the importance of role modelling, social support and parental encouragement as determinants of a child's future activity habits. Woolger and Power (1993) list five ways in which there is a connection between social learning and sports participation:

- Acceptance and social support

- Providing models

- Expressing expectations

- Strengthening behaviour by rewarding and punishing

- Controlling behaviour and giving detailed instructions (pp. 171–189).

Parents also control important aspects of the physical environment that can affect children's physical activity such as access to facilities, equipment and sport and recreation programmes. Eccles and Harold (1991) advocate an expectancy socialisation approach rather than focusing on parental behaviour. Their expectancy value model of achievement, choice and behaviour proposes that children's motivational-related cognitions (e.g. perceived competence, value of involvement) are shaped through interaction with their parents. In their view, parents in particular are presumed to influence children's judgement by communicating their own beliefs about the child's likelihood of success and the relative value of the various achievement areas.

In the available literature, it appears clear that there is significant familial resemblance of physical activity habits (Moore et al., 1991; Freedson and Evenson, 1991; Canada Fitness Survey, 1981; Perusse et al., 1989). Gottlieb and Chen (1985) compared the activity patterns of 2,695 students in 52 schools against their parents. They found that

> the strong relationship found between parental exercise
> and that of the child implicates parental modelling of exer-
> cise as a mechanism in the socialisation of the children's
> lifestyle behaviour (p. 537).

Freedson and Evenson (1991) confirmed a strong and positive relationship between parental and child physical activity levels. They found that, in particular, children for whom both parents were categorised as active were six times as likely to be active than children for whom both parents were inactive.

While it seems clear that parents influence their children's physical activity, differences between the relative influence of fathers and mothers upon children's activity socialisation have been highlighted in a number of studies. Research by Carson et al. (1993) concluded that fathers have more physical contact with infant sons than with infant daughters, and engage in more rough-and-tumble play with their sons than with their daughters. In outlining the results of the UK National Children and Youth Fitness Survey (NCYFS II), Ross et al. (1987) stated that while mothers exercise with equal frequency with sons and daughters, fathers were shown to spend much more time exercising with sons. Lewko and Greendorfer (1988) also agree that fathers appear to play the primary role in influencing both boys and girls to participate in sports. Williams (1993) suggests that fathers in particular are more likely to play physical games with their sons than they are with their daughters. However, Weiss and Bredemeier (1983) suggest that parents are often more encouraging of their son's involvement in physical activity than of their daughter's involvement.

In their research, Yang et al. (1996) found that the physical activity levels of mothers had little association with the physical activity of the boys and only a weak association with the sports participation of the girls. Running counter to these findings, however, Perusse et al. (1989) found no differences in the mother–child and father–child correlation, while Sallis et al. (1988) found a stronger mother–child activity correlation than father–child correlation. However, a possible explanation for the findings of Sallis et al. (1988) may relate to the fact that nearly twice as many mothers provided information as fathers.

Despite these data supporting the influence of the family on children's physical activity, Greendorfer and Ewing (1994) state that parental influence studies have provided only limited advances in the understanding of how children either become involved or remain involved in physical activities. Sallis et al. (1988) and Brustad (1993a) specifically highlight the fact that the specific mechanisms of influence in relation to familial aggregation have just begun to be studied. It is therefore important to understand the mechanisms of influence within the family.

Role modelling is one possible explanation for the relationship between parents and children's activity levels. In assessing the potential for physical activity modelling effects with the family, the role of parental physical activity patterns and parental exercise with children must be examined. Ross et al. (1987) considered that exercise habits of parents could be expected to affect children through a modelling effect or other means. They also suggest that the frequency with which mothers and fathers exercise with their children may communicate to the child something about the parental value associated with exercise, and therefore children of parents who engage in regular physical activity will also be physically active. Freedson and Evenson (1991) confirmed this view that parents' and children's physical activity are positively correlated by stating that "physical activity among children may be increased by promoting physical activity among parents" (p. 338).

The findings from the 1991 Young People's Leisure and Lifestyle study, a major longitudinal study of 10,000 Scottish young people, acknowledge the influence parents have on their children's participation in competitive sport. Over one-third of boys aged between 13 and 16 years reported that they participated in competitive sports because their parents wanted them to. However, the corresponding figure for girls was lower, with less than a quarter of girls reporting that they participated in competitive sports to please their parents. The gender difference may be explained by the gender socialisation research. Several writers have shown that parents are often more encouraging of their son's involvement than of their daughter's involvement (McPherson et al., 1989; Coakley, 1996; Greendorfer and Lewko, 1988; Williams, 1993; Weiss and Breidemeier, 1983). Williams (1993) also suggests that fathers are more likely to play physical games and sports with their sons than with their daughters. Boys are also socialised to play outdoor games and girls are encouraged more towards indoor activities (Hendry et al., 1993; Van Wersch, 1997). Similarly, girls are also not given as much freedom to participate in casual activities as boys and are more likely to be accompanied by a parent when they are at an activity (McPherson et al., 1989). Therefore, through the socialisation process, it can be expected that the type, amount and range of activities engaged in by girls and boys will be different.

An important point which emerges from the literature is that parental support has a positive connection with the pleasure and interest that the child takes in sport (Power and Woolger, 1994; Weiss and Hayashi, 1995; Woolger and Power, 1993). The corollary also appears to be true, i.e. that parents' negative attitudes and behaviour correlate negatively with children's enjoyment of sport. As enjoyment appears to be the main reason why participants right across the spectrum take part in sport, the parental support role may be a key determinant as to whether or not the adolescent will take part and remain active in sport. Researchers have also found some differences in parental expectations in relation to competitive sports participation. Parental expectation of those children who compete in sport appear to be more demanding than those whose children participate for fun. Hellstedt (1990), in a study of thirteen-year-old slalom skiers, found that the majority of the youths felt that their parents really pushed them into competing. It has also been found that the parents of competitive swimmers are more demanding than the parents of children who swim for exercise (Purdy, Eitzen and Haufler, 1982).

There is little available research concerning the influences of single-parent families on sports participation. This is surprising, as the changing nature of the family is a major social trend. A report by *The Sunday Times* (October 1998) estimates the number of children currently being raised in non-nuclear families at 40 per cent and the trend is for this number to increase. In Ireland, the percentage of children registered as born to single mothers has risen dramatically in recent years, as can be seen in Table 7.1 below.

Table 7.1: Children Born to Unmarried Mothers in Ireland

Year	% of Children Born to Unmarried Mothers
1985	9%
1990	15%
1997	26%
1999	35%

Source: Central Statistics Office, Dublin.

Coakley (1987) in his research found that children from single-parent families had fewer opportunities to involve themselves in sporting activities. However, one study which was carried out by Yang et al. (1996) contradicted Coakley's findings. They found that the percentage of children with single parents who participated in sports club activities was actually higher than of those with passive fathers and even of those with moderate activity fathers. They made an interesting claim that "to promote children's participation in sport, no father is better than a passive father" (p. 286). This may indicate the negative influence of a passive father or it may be that many single mothers try to compensate for the lack of a father.

Chapter 8

PRESENTATION AND ANALYSIS OF SURVEY FINDINGS

This chapter presents the main findings from a systematic analysis of the data obtained from questionnaires completed by 3,315 adolescents in full-time second-level education. These data are presented in two main sections:

1. The first section offers a comprehensive data set on the leisure and lifestyle patterns of adolescents in Waterford City. This includes information not just about their sporting and physical activity interests but also in relation to their involvement in youth groups, their drinking and smoking habits and their pursuit of some other leisure activities such as computer games.

2. The second section deals specifically with two key areas that are likely to influence the physical activity patterns of adolescents. Firstly, there is an analysis of factors that influence socialisation into sport itself (antecedents). Secondly, the factors that encourage participation or drop out from sport are then considered (drivers and constraints). The aim of this section is to illustrate some general trends that are further analysed in the qualitative research.

As well as presenting and analysing data in relation to the leisure and lifestyle patterns of adolescents, the process of working through this substantial data set had another key function. Quantitative data can help identify issues and trends but are much less useful in explaining the specific nature and detail of the issues they raise. It was expected therefore that the data set

would pose interesting questions that could usefully be explored in the interview research. The findings from these interviews are presented in the next chapter.

LEISURE AND LIFESTYLE PATTERNS

This section aims to give an overview of some of the sporting,
leisure and lifestyle patterns of a cohort of adolescents. There
are many complexities involved in the process of assessing and
describing the *typical* adolescent's lifestyle and the results from
a written questionnaire are particularly useful in quantifying
elements of that lifestyle. The data from the questionnaires also
throw up some interesting trends and unexpected turns and the
more salient ones are outlined. There are several other issues
that remain unresolved, some of which are earmarked for further analysis in the interview research. Leisure time for the adolescent is the period when many different lifestyles and leisure
activities can be tried and exchanged (Hendry et al., 1993).
Adolescents appear to have many choices and this analysis attempts to portray what adolescents say they do in their leisure
time. The first area of interest that is explored is their sporting
involvement.

General Findings about Sports Participation

- A total of 27 per cent (n = 877) of those surveyed claimed
  not to take part in any sport. This appears to be a high figure
  considering that adolescence is the time when there is the
  greatest opportunity to participate in sports over the course
  of the life cycle (Hendry et al., 1993).

- The influence of school provision is significant in facilitating
  certain adolescents to play sports, particularly team sports.
  Forty per cent of all team sports are played in school whilst
  eleven per cent of individual sports are played in the school
  setting. The implication here is that the school's PE programme is dominated by team sports. This was borne out
  when the figures were analysed for where the adolescents
  played their individual sports. Of the total of 2,523 who participated in individual sports, only 282 of these played in

school. This represents a surprisingly low figure of 11 per cent. This poses a question, particularly for girls. If girls are more interested in individual than team sports (Van Wersch, 1997), as the results of this research show, are schools catering for their needs?

- When considering whether the activities took place in an indoor or outdoor setting, the research found that two-thirds (67 per cent) of the sports played were outdoor sports with one-third being indoors (33 per cent). There was also a strong gender difference between participation in outdoor and indoor sport by boys and girls as illustrated in Table 8.1 below.

Table 8.1: Gender Differences in Participation for Indoor and Outdoor Sports

	Indoor	**Outdoor**
Males	22%	78%
Females	49%	51%

(n=3,315)

Research (Emmett, 1971; Kremer et al., 1997; Mason, 1995; Hendry et al., 1993) suggests that girls are socialised more into indoor activities than boys and this appears to be confirmed by the above figures. As far back as 1978, Frith talks about the "culture of the bedroom" as being significant for adolescent girls. This theme of girls spending more time pursing indoor activities is also documented by McPherson et al. (1989) and Lewko and Greendorfer (1988). Larson (1995) highlighted the importance of the privacy and interaction within the bedroom for girls' emotional development. Boys, on the other hand, clearly appear to be socialised into outdoor sports as evidenced by almost a four-to-one bias of outdoor as opposed to indoor sports.

Participation in Team Sports

Any respondents who played team sport(s) had the opportunity to list up to three team sports they played. The participation rates are summarised in Table 8.2 below.

Table 8.2: Participation Rates in Team Sports

	Participants	Non-participants
Total (n = 3,288)	56%	44%
Boys (n = 1,813)	64%	36%
Girls (n = 1,475)	46%	54%

Over half (56 per cent) of the respondents surveyed participated in at least one team sport. However, there are clear gender differences in participation levels. Whilst almost two-thirds of boys play team sports, less than half of the surveyed girls reported being involved in team sports.

Table 8.3: Team Sports Participated in

Total (n = 3,316)	%	Male (n = 2,073)	%	Female (n = 1,063)	%
1. Soccer	27%	1. Soccer	36%	1. Basketball	34%
2. Football*	17%	2. Football*	21%	2. Hockey	22%
3. Basketball	17%	3. Hurling	19%	3. Soccer	15%
4. Hurling	13%	4. Rugby	12%	4. Camogie	12%
5. Hockey	9%	5. Basketball	6%	5. Volleyball	7%
6. Rugby	8%	6. Hockey	3%	6. Football	5%
7. Camogie	4%	7. Others	2%	7. Others	5%
8. Volleyball	3%				
9. Rounders	1%				
10. Others	2%				

* "Football" here refers to Gaelic football.

As can be seen in Table 8.3 above, the number of sports that were mentioned was surprisingly small. Four sports accounted for 74 per cent of the team sports played. Soccer was the most popular team sport. It is also the only sport that got a top 3 ranking for both boys and girls. Soccer ranked first for boys and third for girls. There is a marked gender differentiation in a number of the sports that are played. Basketball and hockey were the favourites with girls whilst soccer, Gaelic football and hurling dominated amongst the boys. The dominance of soccer, which is almost as popular with boys as Gaelic football and hurling combined (27 per cent play soccer as against 33 per cent football and hurling combined), may confirm a perceived sharp decline in the relative popularity of what are often termed the traditional Irish sports. The high media profile and in particular the saturation of certain satellite channels with English soccer allied to the recent success of the Irish international soccer team may have contributed to the increasing popularity of soccer. There has also been a domino effect in that girls' participation rates in soccer have mushroomed to 15 per cent. This reflects the changing social nature of sport, as girls would not have been playing soccer until relatively recently. In Ireland, the Women's Football Association of Ireland (WFAI) was founded in 1973 and, according to a spokeswoman for the FAI, it was not until the early 1990s that women's soccer became popular in Ireland.[1]

Participation in Individual Sports

Table 8.4: Participation in Individual Sports

	Participants	Non-participants	
Total	50%	50%	(n = 3,251)
Boys	47%	53%	(n = 1,782)
Girls	53%	47%	(n = 1,469)

From examining Table 8.4 above, it can be seen that in overall terms there were fewer participants in individual as opposed to team sports. However, an interesting finding from these figures

---

[1] From an interview with Mairéad Collins, Irish Schoolgirls Soccer Development Officer.

is that girls, on a pro-rata basis of respondents, are more active than boys. This may reflect the fact that boys are more attracted than girls to the competitive (Sallis, 1994) and physical nature (McPherson et al., 1989) of many team sports. Girls appear to opt more for recreational and social activities such as swimming, horse riding, dance, jogging and aerobics (Hendry et al., 1993).

Table 8.5: Individual Sports Participated in

Total		Male		Female	
1. Swimming	18%	1. Swimming	14%	1. Swimming	23%
2. Tennis	10%	2. Tennis	10%	2. Tennis	10%
3. Athletics	8%	3. Pitch & Putt	9%	3. Athletics	8%
4. Cycling	8%	4. Cycling	9%	4. Cycling	8%
5. Badminton	5%	5. Golf	8%	5. Horse Riding	7%
6. Pitch & Putt	5%	6. Athletics	7%	6. Badminton	6%
7. Golf	5%	7. Snooker	5%	7. Aerobics	4%
8. Horse Riding	4%	8. Badminton	5%	8. Jogging	4%
9. Pool	3%	9. Fishing	4%	9. Lifesaving	3%
10. Jogging	3%	10. Pool	4%	10. Dance	3%
11. Snooker	3%	11. Weight Lifting	3%	11. Weight Lifting	2%
12. Martial Arts	2%	12. Squash	2%	12. Irish Dance	2%
13. Fishing	2%	13. Martial Arts	2%	13. Canoeing	2%
14. Canoeing	2%	14. Boxing	2%	14. Go Karting	2%
15. Weight Lifting	2%	15. Lifesaving	2%	15. Gymnastics	2%
16. Lifesaving	2%	16. Horse Riding	2%	16. Pool	2%
17. Squash	2%	17. Jogging	2%	17. Martial Arts	1%
18. Aerobics	2%	18. Other	10%	18. Other	11%
19. Dance	2%				
20. Other	12%				

(n = 3,251)

On analysis of the most popular individual sports, as shown in Table 8.5 above, the same two sports, swimming and tennis, rank first and second for both genders. However, the clear dominance of swimming for girls is worth noting. One possible reason for this is that swimming may be considered a *gender-appropriate* activity for girls, i.e. girls may be socialised more into swimming in primary school than boys. A study of usage of the local swimming pools shows that girls' primary schools use swimming pools twice as much as boys primary schools (Connor, 1997). There are a number of possible reasons for this. Swimming is a popular activity that is relatively easy to organise. If the teachers are not confident to teach swimming themselves, they can avail of swimming instructors from the pool. The perceived gender-appropriate nature of swimming may appeal to girls' schools more than sports such as soccer or camogie. Another factor may be the compensatory nature of girls being offered swimming because some teachers feel that boys' sporting needs are adequately catered for with team sports and, as a result, they seek other appropriate activities for girls whose needs are not being met.

Gender stereotyping appears prevalent amongst some sports. Certain sports in the survey returns are exclusive to girls and others to boys. Aerobics, dance, Irish dancing and gymnastics are exclusive to girls whilst pitch and putt, golf, fishing and boxing are only in the male domain. Whilst some of these sports, such as boxing and aerobics, could be expected to be dominated by a single gender due to homophobic and gender stereotyping (Cahn, 1994), there may be more subtle agencies at work which may make sports such as golf and pitch and putt appear inaccessible to girls. Possible reasons could be the lack of suitable role models for girls. Gallagher in her PhD study (1997) points out that 65 per cent of women golfers in Ireland are over 35 years old. She is of the view therefore that adolescent girls lack identifiable role models. In their minds, golf is in the main a sport that their mothers play. Thus, girls in this instance may be less likely than boys to try out some activities such as golf. Whatever the reasons, it would appear obvious that there is gender stereotyping in relation to participation levels by boys and girls in certain sports.

Time Spent Playing Sport

Table 8.6: Time Spent Playing Sport

Male (n = 1,543)			Female (n = 1,051)		
Hours Spent	*%*	*Number*	*Hours Spent*	*%*	*Number*
1-5	43	664	1-5	47	492
6-10	27	422	6-10	39	406
11-15	15	224	11-15	9	96
16-19	7	104	16-19	3	29
20+	8	129	20+	2	28

The time spent playing sport is summarised in Table 8.6 above. In the main, boys are more active and for a greater amount of time. The main finding here is that the more active participants (>10 hours per week on sport) tend to be male. However, there are a cohort of girls (14 per cent) who appear highly committed to their sporting endeavours. These girls participate for over 10 hours per week. In percentage terms, over double this amount (30 per cent) of the boys participate at this level. As well as being generally more active, the highest dedicated sports people in terms of time spent on sport, also appear more likely to be male than female. Whilst 5 per cent of girls claim to spend more than 15 hours per week on sport, three times that number of males (15 per cent) claim to spend this amount of time at their sports.

Level of Sports Representation

A high percentage of adolescents (60 per cent) have represented their school or club in some sport. As there is a diverse range of local and school sports and activities played, this indicates that many schools and clubs have been successful in attracting the adolescents to play for them. However, these figures may be misleading, as they give no indication as to the level of commitment given by the participants. For example, taking part in the Community Games may mean just one outing a year to represent a local area for those involved. To gain some indication of the level of activity, their level of representation (for the 60 per cent who participated) was ranked and these results are shown in Figure 8.1 below.

Figure 8.1: Highest Level of Sports Representation

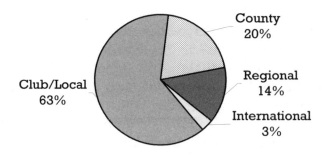

(n = 1,895)

Participation figures at the higher levels (i.e. at regional or international level) appear high. However, there may be a number of explanations for this. Waterford is the main city in the South East Region. Because the population is relatively low, it means that adolescents in this region may have a higher chance of regional representation than, for example, Dublin or Cork teenagers. Thus, 14 per cent of active adolescents have had the opportunity to represent their region, and a further 3 per cent have represented their country. Some of the sports where Irish representation has been achieved include basketball, athletics, boxing, soccer, golf, swimming, gymnastics and badminton. Waterford appears to be a particularly strong base for a number of these sports and this is reflected in the success achieved at national levels. For example, in national league basketball, the ladies team (Wildcats) were the most successful team in Ireland during the 1990s. One girls' school in Waterford appears to act as a feeder to the Wildcats. The club have trained and played their home matches in their sports hall for several years. The pupils in this school would therefore be repeatedly exposed to strong role models and many of the team players also coach the school's basketball teams. It was the view of one of the school's teachers that "many aspiring players would choose to attend this school because of our basketball tradition".

Non-Sport Leisure Participation

In order to establish overall leisure patterns, as well as sports participation, adolescents were asked about their membership (if applicable) of any group or organisation outside of sport. Examples of such groups included the scouts, youth clubs, bands and other youth organisations. The research also tried to establish some benchmarks of the non-sporting leisure and lifestyle patterns of the adolescents outside of their involvement in organised groups. Such activities included their television-watching habits, their reading habits and their hobbies. Other areas of interest were whether or not they smoked or drank and if they worked. These questions attempted to gain an insight into the nature of adolescents' lives. Many of these issues, such as time spent working would be expected to impact directly on the time available for other physical activities. Similarly, it was hoped that their answers would throw some light on the values placed on differing lifestyle choices by adolescents. For example, were adolescents interested in youth organisations and, if so, what was the level of interest?

Youth Club Membership

A small percentage of Waterford adolescents are members of youth clubs, as shown in Table 8.6 below. This is despite the fact that there are several youth clubs in the city which claim to welcome new members. Another interesting point to note is that adolescents are members of youth clubs primarily in their early school years at second-level. There is a severe dropout rate from the end of second year in particular. Youth clubs only seem to appeal to first- and second-year adolescents (Hendry et al., 1993) while Table 8.7 shows the gender balance from youth club members to be reasonably level. Clearly few young people are attracted to youth clubs despite their availability. Bone (1982) has suggested that acceptance patterns are related to social class in that early school leavers are less likely to attend organised clubs offering sporting interests or hobbies or being in a uniformed service such as the Order of Malta. Hendry et al. (1993) suggest that the reason why many adolescents do not attend such organisations is because they are closely linked with the school's organisational structure or because of the pattern of discipline or because school buildings are used. Adolescents as they grow older tend to move from structured to casual leisure (Coleman and Hendry, 1990) and as a result many reject the disciplined and structured nature of many youth clubs.

Table 8.7: Youth Club Membership by Gender

Yes	No
15%	85%
Boys: 8% (n = 254)	
Girls: 7% (n = 223)	

(n = 3,237)

Membership of Community/Charity Groups

As Table 8.8 shows, girls appear more likely to join a community or charity group than boys. The gender breakdown is almost two girls for every boy taken on a percentage basis. There are a number of possible reasons why girls dominate these organisations. One possibility is that girls are more likely to be socialised into the caring and social professions. In Ireland today, women dominate the general nursing profession, and current female national teacher graduates outnumber males by eight to one. Membership of organisations like the Red Cross or the St Vincent De Paul may be a step in this socialisation process. In addition to this, parents may be more protective of their daughters and prefer to have them involved in structured organisations (McPherson et al., 1989). The indoor nature of these activities may also appeal more to girls than boys, who may be more attracted to organisations such as the Scouts, which have a more outdoor ethos.

Table 8.8: Community/Charity Group Membership by Gender

Yes	No
11%	89%
Boys: 4% (n=126)	
Girls: 7% (n=216)	

(n = 3,121)

Whilst they appear to have limited appeal for many adolescents, there are however, a wide variety of community and charity groups. Over twenty organisations have members from the adolescent student community. From the details in Table 8.9 below, a number of interesting points emerge.

Table 8.9: Community/Charity Groups with Most Membership

Peace and Justice Group	10%
President's Award	7%
Scouts	7%
Community Games	6%
Civil Defence	6%
Order of Malta	4%
Special Olympics	4%
St Vincent De Paul	3%
Red Cross	3%
FCA	3%
Girl Guides	3%
Group Link	3%
Manor of St John	3%

(n = 3,121)

Firstly, unlike youth clubs, membership of these organisations spans the full range of second-level school attendance. There are a number of possible explanations for this. Some of the organisations have an older age requirement.[2] As a result, many of these organisations may have an adult ethos that may appeal to older adolescents. Secondly, a number of these organisations have links through the schools' Transition Year programmes. The Transition Year is the first year of the senior

---

[2] The Civil Defence, for example, have an age requirement of sixteen years. Interestingly, the Scouts also have an upper age limit of sixteen. Above that, they can belong as volunteers but the transition is not smooth due to the shortage of suitable leaders.

cycle in school and adolescents who get involved during this year may retain membership as they continue their schooling.

Membership of Social or Cultural Organisations

In summarising the adolescent involvement in youth groups, there were in total 36 groups with which some adolescents were involved. The gender split amongst those who were members was almost even. It is evident that adolescents may have the opportunity of becoming part of a diverse range of possible groups. However, it can be seen that all the various organisations including youth clubs, community and youth groups and social and cultural groups (as shown in Table 8.11 below) only attracted to their membership a minority of adolescents. The majority of adolescents (65 per cent) do not appear to be interested in being involved in an organised youth group and this suggests that the peer group and non-formal groups hold the greatest appeal for most adolescents.

Table 8.10: Membership of Social or Cultural Organisations

Yes	No
9%	91%
Boys 4% (n=123)	
Girls 5% (n=153)	

(n = 3,078)

Table 8.11: Social or Cultural Organisations with Most Membership

Social Clubs	15%
Scouts	11%
Sports and Social Clubs	10%
Foróige	8%
Community Groups	7%

(n = 3,078)

Consumption of Alcohol

Drinking alcoholic beverage appears to be a popular leisure activity among adolescents. Half of the interviewees *claim* to drink at least once a month (see Figure 8.2 below). Whilst it is illegal to consume alcohol before one's eighteenth birthday, this legislation does not appear to be strictly enforced. Teenagers appear to have little difficulty in either being served in bars or in securing drink from off-licences. The popularity of drinking as a leisure activity is evidenced by the fact that a third of all those surveyed claimed to drink at least once a week.

Figure 8.2: Claimed Alcoholic Drinking Patterns of Adolescents

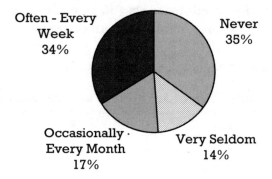

Often - Every Week 34%

Never 35%

Occasionally · Every Month 17%

Very Seldom 14%

(n = 3,145)

The Department of Health and Children launched a major study titled *The National Health and Lifestyle Surveys* in early 1999. It is worth noting their first strategy in relation to alcohol consumption is "to promote moderation in the consumption of alcohol and to reduce the risks to physical, mental and family health that can arise from alcohol misuse" (p. 24). If they were to be successful with this strategy, it would appear that they would need to target a significant amount of their resources to tackling the problem of underage drinking.

Smoking

Figure 8.3: The Numbers who Smoked a Full Cigarette in the Past Week

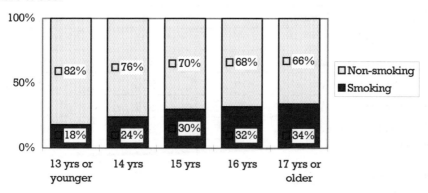

(n = 3,194)

Figure 8.3 above suggests that smoking is a prevalent activity with over a quarter of adolescents claiming to have smoked in the previous week. There are no significant gender differences as regards cigarette smoking. Smoking rates increase with age from 18 per cent in the first year of school rising to over a third (34 per cent) by the final year of second-level schooling. Possible reasons for this increase may include:

- Having more money

- Being in situations, e.g. bars, where smoking is more prevalent

- Less censure from parents and significant others

- Adopting what appears to be more of an adult role

- Greater influence of peer pressure.

Hobbies

The following are the favourite hobbies categorised by degree of popularity. Each adolescent nominated their three favourite hobbies and the results are as shown in Table 8.12 below.

Table 8.12: Main Hobbies

Hobby	Number	As % of Total
1. Listening to music	909	12
2. Watching television	862	11
3. Cinema	801	10
4. Computer games	665	9
5. Playing music	655	8
6. Reading	577	7
7. Visiting friends	572	7
8. Art	399	5
9. Sports spectator	249	3
10. Walking	215	3
11. Looking after pets	182	2
12. Collecting items	170	2
13. Drama	141	2
14. Board games	115	1

(n = 7,724)

The teenagers are interested in a wide diversity of hobbies and the above fourteen favourite hobbies still only represent 82 per cent of the choices. Technology and mass media activities dominate their interests. The top choices also reflect passive hobbies, where the adolescent is being entertained rather than being active, creative or interactive. There are few gender differences in choices and the only particularly gender-based hobby is looking after pets which is far more popular with girls than boys. Going to the cinema is a popular teenage activity.

Playing Computer Games

With the increasing availability of personal computers both at home and in school, this research attempted to establish if the playing of computer games ranked highly on the list of leisure activities. Whilst computer games include consoles such as Playstation which does not require a computer, many computer games are now played on home computers. Computers are often purchased for their educational value by parents. Gillard (1995) claims that children and teenagers are key motivational influences in the purchase of computers because parents felt that they were educational necessities for their children. Their greatest actual usage for adolescents may be as a means of playing computer games. Computers are widely available in homes, schools, libraries and in amusement arcades.

Figure 8.4: Playing Computer Games

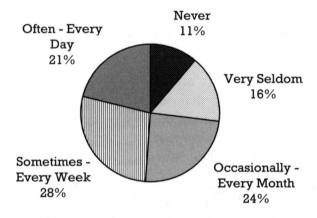

(n = 3,212)

As can be seen in Figure 8.4 above, playing computer games appears to be a popular activity amongst adolescents. In fact, only 11 per cent say that they never play computer games. Over one-fifth (21 per cent) play every day. However, the early indications from this research would appear to confirm the international trends of increasing home-based and technology-based leisure. Many analysts predict that the greatest challenge to participation in physical activity lies in the competition from home-based entertainment. With the increasing technology and sophistication of what is available to provide entertainment to adolescents, it appears that the competition from home-based entertainment will become more intense in the coming years.

Televisions in Adolescents' Homes

Practically all of the homes in Waterford City have at least one television set, as shown in Table 8.13 below.

Table 8.13: Homes with at Least One Television

Yes	No
99.67%	0.33%

(n = 3,315)

The small number of homes that don't have a television set may be the result of a decision made by parents rather than solely being an issue of cost. Most of the houses with no television sets appear to be in the more affluent areas. Parents may have made a decision to bring up their children without the television influence that they feel dominates many homes. However, the key point is that only a tiny minority of adolescents do not have access to a television in their homes.

Television Channels Available

Of the 3,214 homes with televisions, the following are examples of the television channels available:

- RTE 1 and RTE 2 — 100 per cent
- BBC channels — 96 per cent
- Sky Sports — 30 per cent
- All cable channels — 21 per cent.

Adolescents have significant choice in their television viewing. There appears to be a greater likelihood that extra channels will be subscribed to in the working-class areas. This is particularly the case with Sky Sports, which has achieved significant market penetration. This may impact as one of the reasons for the popularity of soccer among the adolescents in the City. Many of the homes in the working-class areas also appear to have the cable channels. The BBC channels are widely available and as a result, teenagers in Waterford may be watching the same programmes as teenagers in British cities like Liverpool, Glasgow or London. The British media appear to be widely watched and this hints at the potential globalising effects of television (O'Toole, 1997).

How Often Adolescents Watched Television

Given the wide availability both of television sets and the variety of channels available, it is not surprising to find that television viewing is a major leisure activity among adolescents. Only 4 per cent of adolescents do not watch television with any regularity. Television is therefore a potentially major influence on the lives of adolescents, as summarised in Figure 8.5 below.

Figure 8.5: How Often Adolescents Watched Television

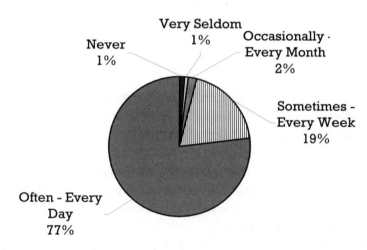

(n = 3,276)

Library Usage

This question was attempting to establish how many adolescents were using the library services that are available. Library usage was also expected to give an indication of how often adolescents read during their leisure time. The figure for library usage as shown in Figure 8.6 was just over one-third (36 per cent). Only 8 per cent claim to have used the library on a weekly basis. The remaining 2,000 adolescents claimed not to

have made any use of their local library in the month prior to
the survey.

Figure 8.6: Library Usage (in the previous month)

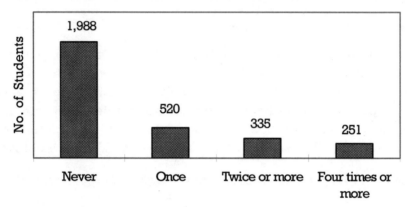

(n = 3,094)

Time Spent Working

There were two areas under investigation here. Firstly, how
much time if any, was being spent at work whilst adolescents
were in full-time education. Secondly, whether there was any
link between social class and work patterns. The work referred
to was for paid employment outside the home. The type of work
involved was predominately baby-sitting, supermarket or bar
work, amusement arcades, petrol attendants and fast-food out-
lets (not in any rank order).

As can be seen in Figure 8.7 below, almost two-thirds (64
per cent) did not work. There are a number of possible reasons
for this. Firstly, they may not have wanted work. Similarly, they
may not have been allowed to work either by their parents or
by state law. On the other hand, there may not be enough available work to satisfy the demands of the adolescents. Of those
who worked, 14 per cent did so for 11 hours or more with a
small percentage working over 20 hours per week. These
adolescents were primarily from the senior cycle of the second-
level school system and were predominately from working-
class areas. One possible reason could be that in many cases
adolescents from middle-class areas are being encouraged to

concentrate on their schooling whilst in working-class areas, there may be pressure to bring additional money into the household.

Figure 8.7: Time Spent Working

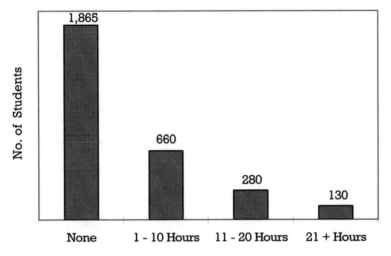

(n = 2,935)

Family Size

Family size is one factor which will impact on the likelihood of sports participation (McPherson et al., 1989). Children who have no siblings are more likely to get more opportunities for sports participation. Similarly, they are more likely to be socialised into individual sports. The sizes of the families to which the respondents belong were thus analysed and the results are shown in Table 8.14 below. Whilst the trend in Ireland is heading towards the European Union norm (1.6 children), this does not appear to be reflected currently in the family sizes for adolescents surveyed in Waterford City. The mean family size in Waterford City is 3.68.

Some interesting facts emerge from these figures. Firstly, just 129 teenagers in the sample have no siblings. This appears low and may in part be attributed to Catholic values in Irish society and the trend towards larger families in Catholic countries. Equally, it could be an issue related to relative economic standing. Secondly, at the other extreme, there are a number of very large families. A total of 26 per cent of the children surveyed were from families of five children or more. The mean family size of 3.68 in Waterford City is well above both the European and American averages.

Table 8.14: Breakdown of Family Sizes

No. of Children	No. of Families with this Number	Represented as % of Total
1	129	4%
2	657	20%
3	933	29%
4	695	21%
5	423	13%
6	181	6%
7	89	3%
8	64	2%
9 or more	33	2%

(n = 3,216)

ANTECEDENTS TO SPORTS PARTICIPATION

Overview

This section examines two fundamental areas in youth sport. Firstly, how are young people introduced to sport? The socialisation process into sport and the impact of role modelling are both examined in this section.[3] Secondly, what kinds of factors encourage teenagers to stay involved? Similarly what kinds of barriers prevent them from being (more) involved in sports? There are a wide variety of factors that will drive or constrain young people to participate in sport. The key drivers are outlined and are generally found to be intrinsic in nature. The barriers to sport

---

[3] Socialisation has been defined as an active process of learning and social development that occurs as people interact with one another and become acquainted with the social world in which they live as they form ideas about who they are and make decisions about their goals and behaviours (McPherson et al, 1989).

facility usage are then highlighted in an attempt to understand why adolescents do not use available sports facilities.

Introduction to Sport

The survey findings suggest that there was no particular age band when adolescents were introduced to their first-named sport. There was almost an equal number introduced each year between the ages of five and twelve, the primary school years. However, 71 per cent had experience of their first-named sport by the age of nine. This suggests that the primary school years are particularly important in the early socialisation into particular sports.

An analysis of who introduced the adolescent to their first-named sport shows that school was mentioned most often (25 per cent), followed by friends (22 per cent), father (19 per cent), club (17 per cent), mother (9 per cent) and brother or sister (8 per cent). Interestingly, when grouped together, the influence of the family is of particular significance, accounting for 37 per cent of the introductions. This would appear to confirm the influence of the family as the key agent of socialisation during the primary school years (McPherson et al., 1989).

This information was analysed to cross-check if adolescents were socialised through the same routes into their favourite hobbies. There were some interesting differences in how adolescents were introduced to their hobbies as opposed to their sports, as can be seen in Table 8.15 below.

Table 8.15: How Adolescents were Introduced to their Sports and Hobbies

	Sports	Hobbies
By a family member	36%	26%
By a teacher	25%	10%
By a friend	22%	28%
Got involved themselves	—	36%
Club	17%	—

(n = 6,826)

What is noticeable about these results is that adolescents appear to be reasonably self-reliant in getting involved in hobbies either through their own volition or through their peers (64 per cent). The influence of family and school is less influential for their hobbies than for sport. One possible explanation for this is that many of the hobbies may have been taken up since they became adolescents. For example, hobbies like going to the cinema or listening to music would be expected to be more prevalent amongst adolescents than younger children. At this stage of their development, adolescents are less influenced by the school and parents while the peer group becomes the key socialising agency (Hendry et al., 1993).

Other socialising agents were also examined. When the adolescents were asked who else in the family played sports, some interesting trends emerged. Whilst 71 per cent of the sample said their father played sport, only 31 per cent claimed that their mother played. It appears clear that for the adolescents' parents generation, there was a clear link between gender and the likelihood of playing sports. With a mean family size of just under four, many of their mothers' time for sport may have been curtailed.

Interestingly, the majority of the fathers played GAA sports (48 per cent) with only 13 per cent being involved in soccer. This points to an inter-generational increase in the popularity of soccer (27 per cent) amongst the adolescents. The activity of golf is also high, with 18 per cent of fathers currently being active in golf. This sport would appear to have an adult ethos, as it is not currently a major interest (5 per cent, almost exclusively male) amongst the adolescents. Of those adolescents who played sports and also had siblings, 89 per cent claimed that their siblings played sports. This appears to indicate the concept of sporting families (De Knop et al., 1996), i.e. if one child is active, the other children are also likely to be active in sports.

DRIVERS AND CONSTRAINTS TO SPORTS PARTICIPATION

This section of the research findings presents an analysis of the significant drivers and constraints to sports participation for adolescents. These are the factors that may be instrumental in determining whether adolescents remain active or drop out from sport. The school plays a particularly important role in relation to providing 40 per cent of all team sports. Sports clubs and associations have an even more important role, catering for 60 per cent of all team sports and 89 per cent of individual sports.

Reasons for Sports Participation

In general, the findings illustrated in Figure 8.8 below show similar trends to results obtained in previous research (Kremer, et al. 1997; Mason, 1995; Hendry et al., 1993). The key motivation for sports participation appears to be based on intrinsic rather than extrinsic factors. There are three main reasons given for participating in sports. Firstly, a significant percentage (37 per cent) of Waterford adolescents play primarily for enjoyment. The influence of the peer group is evidenced in the fact that 28 per cent of them play because their friends play. A fifth of adolescents play to keep fit (21 per cent). This is a reason that becomes more prevalent as adolescents advance through their schooling years. Extrinsic factors motivate only a small minority of the adolescents. For instance, 4 per cent of boys want to go into professional sport, particularly rugby and soccer. It is worth noting that this is a reason that was not given by a single girl who was surveyed. This may reflect the fact that boys, more so than girls, are socialised to be competitive (McPherson et al., 1989). Another gender-based difference was that losing weight was a motivating factor for some of the girls surveyed. This was reported as the primary reason for participation for 6 per cent of girls whilst this was an issue for only 1 per cent of boys. However, it appears clear that "the distinction between intrinsic and extrinsic motivation is clearly significant in terms of physical activity and participation" (van Wersch, 1997, p. 58 in Kremer et al., 1997). The findings from this survey appear to confirm international research, which show that intrinsic motives are the most powerful predictors of future participation and satisfaction (Weiss and Chaumeton, 1992).

Figure 8.8: Reasons for Sports Participation

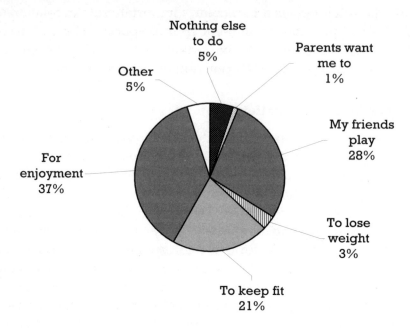

(n = 3,040)

Facilities which are Considered Inaccessible

If adolescents considered facilities inaccessible, then this would be a significant constraint to leisure participation. Whilst there are several leisure facilities available in Waterford, this does not necessarily mean that adolescents feel that they are accessible to them. There are a number of potential reasons why facilities may be considered inaccessible:

• They may be too expensive;

• Adolescents may not feel that they are welcome there;

• Lack of access, e.g. transport available to a facility;

• Unaware of existence of a facility;

• May be afraid to use a facility if it is in a particular area;

• May not have the competence to use a facility, e.g. unable to play golf.

Figure 8.9: Facilities which are Considered Inaccessible

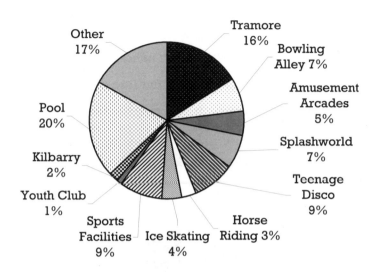

(n = 3,211)

As seen in Figure 8.9 above, the facility which is considered most inaccessible is a swimming pool (20 per cent). As there is no public pool in the city, this is perhaps not surprising. However, the pool that was built by the Waterford Crystal Company fulfils many of the functions of a public swimming pool and is located on the western periphery of the city. The fastest-growing area of the city is on the eastern side, so it is not surprising that many respondents from this side of the city find the pool inaccessible.

Facilities that are Perceived as Needed

When asked about what extra facilities the adolescents would like, this question generated a wide-ranging wish-list but there were some general trends. There appears to be widespread agreement that there are certain facilities that are needed by teenagers. Most of the facilities mentioned are, however, actually *in situ* already.

There are a number of possible reasons why these facilities are mentioned as being needed:

- Lack of knowledge of their availability;
- Over-demand for certain facilities which means they are not available;
- Situated too far away for realistic usage;
- Not making use of their existing facilities;
- Not being made welcome in the current facilities.

Figure 8.10: Facilities that are Perceived as Needed

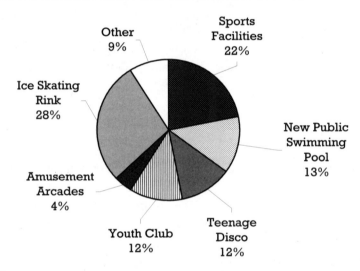

(n = 3,077)

As seen in Figure 8.10 above, the facility which the surveyed population regards as most needed is an ice-skating rink and this finding is consistent across each area of the city surveyed. Given that the only ice-skating rinks in Ireland are in Dublin, this is an unexpected result. A possible reason for this demand could be that there were a number of television programmes which featured adolescents hanging out in ice-skating rinks and this may have *looked cool* to the adolescents.

There was a general desire for more sports facilities and a new pool. If the public facilities were more widely available, e.g. school gymnasia, this could help to alleviate this need. There is a definite perceived need for an additional swimming pool. In real terms, Waterford Glass Pool is not available for school use.[4] There is also an expressed desire for a youth club by 12 per cent of the students. This is surprising, given that there is availability in the existing youth clubs and that they are spread out around the city. Similarly, only 1 per cent expressed a view that youth clubs were inaccessible to them. However, there may be a gap between what is being provided and what the adolescents want. Perhaps they need a different type of youth club which is less structured and provides more activities like youth discos.

SUMMARY OF FINDINGS

From the substantive data set available, there are a number of key findings, which emerge to be of particular interest to this study, and these may be summarised as follows:

- For adolescents, the *higher* your social class grouping, the more likely you are to be an active sports person.

- There is a general decline in participation levels in sport as adolescents get older. This is particularly true for team sports.

- The costs associated with physical activity participation do not appear to be perceived as a major constraint by adolescents.

- Boys are in general more active in sports than girls and for longer periods of time.

- School type is a key determinant to leisure participation.

- Technology and television are the dominant leisure activities for adolescents relative to the amount of time spent at these activities.

- A high percentage of adolescents would appear to drink regularly.

- There is a marked decline in youth club membership as adolescents get older.

---

[4] The availability of the pool to secondary school classes can be as low as four hours per week because of the other demands placed on the pool.

Chapter 9

FINDINGS AND ANALYSIS OF INTERVIEW RESEARCH

The findings from the questionnaire study provided much valuable information in relation to the sporting, leisure and lifestyle patterns of a cohort of adolescents. This research provided a detailed and comprehensive set of statistics in relation to the nature and extent of young people's involvement in sport and physical activity. It also sought to give insights into the factors which motivated individuals to take up and remain active in sport as well as looking at factors which caused adolescents to drop out of sport and physical activity. The research also identified a number of key questions that warranted further research and analysis.

This chapter presents the findings of interviews which addressed these issues and which were carried out primarily with a sub-group of these same adolescents. These interviews have probed directly into the particular decisions made by individual adolescents as to why they choose a particular lifestyle, what they like or dislike about sport and physical activity and, in general, the meaning and importance they attach to what is going on in their world. Each individual will have made their decisions based on a set of unique circumstances, including what kind of facilities they had available, their opportunities for translating their wants into action, the support given to their chosen lifestyle patterns from parents and significant others and any underlying motivations for living a particular lifestyle. For each adolescent, this special set of circumstances will ultimately dictate whether or not they will be physically active. The main aim here is to take an overview of the findings from the data set in an effort to identify trends across a discrete sample of adolescents and to draw inferences that may be applicable to other samples. Another aim will be to portray the intricate details about phenomena such as their feelings, thought processes and emotions in an attempt to understand the meanings or nature of their particular experiences.

The chapter is presented in three sections, essentially as a means of organising and presenting a host of complex and interrelated issues in a more accessible manner. As a result, the analysis is presented under a number of categories for the purpose of clarity. The first section covers the main antecedents to sports participation. This section includes how adolescents were introduced to sport, their views on PE classes and on PE teachers and coaches as well as the influence of role models. The second section then deals with the factors which act as drivers and constraints to participation in physical activity/sport. These include:

- Withdrawal from and aspects of sport which are disliked
- Effects of geographical location
- Facilities
- Favourite and positive aspects of sport
- Time and cost
- Social class groupings and sport
- Gender and sport.

The third section gives an overview of the general lifestyle characteristics as described by a cohort of Irish adolescents. This section examines several areas of their lifestyle, including their smoking and drinking habits, the kinds of things they like doing in their free time, their views on school, and whether or not they work. An understanding of adolescent lifestyle behaviour is of particular importance to people interested in formulating and implementing policies to increase adolescents' sporting involvement.

ANTECEDENTS TO SPORTS PARTICIPATION

Introduction to Sport

If sport and/or physical activity are to become an integral part of an adolescent's lifestyle, much depends on how and when participation begins. The importance of an early introduction to sport is well established (Kremer et al., 1997; McPherson et al., 1989). This section examines what the adolescents who were interviewed remember about their introduction to sport. The key agencies of early socialisation figure highly in the ways adolescents claim to remember being introduced to sport.

Playing with a parent (usually the father) at an early age often leads to a lifelong love of a particular sport. The following quote from a seventeen-year-old male reflects this sentiment: "From an early age, I used to play hurling and football out in the garden every day after school. I have loved it from then on. . . . I was born with it in me . . . life wouldn't be the same without it."

Adolescents are often keenly aware that their parents' interests can reflect a strong cultural tradition in a local area. One fourteen-year-old female noted that "it was a tradition, it was in the family. Everyone in my family and area either played hurling or camogie."

There was sometimes a gender difference evident in the different sports that their father introduced them to as opposed to their mother. One seventeen-year-old female remarked that "my mother influenced me to go horse riding and my father pushed me more towards Gaelic games". It is also interesting to note that this was the only reply by an adolescent who replied first about her mother's influence when questioned about their parental influence in introducing them to sport. It was the norm that the father's influence would be mentioned first. This would appear to confirm the views of Carson et al. (1993) and Greendorfer (1983), amongst others, that fathers as opposed to mothers appear to play the primary role in socialising both boys and girls into sport. In some cases, adolescents were so immersed into an activity through parental modelling that they were always likely to play the same sports as their parents. One fourteen-year-old female, who played camogie, described her parents as being deeply committed to Gaelic games when she said: "My parents are both big in the GAA. My father is manager of a few teams and my mother helps out with some of the functions to raise money."

As the adolescent approaches second-level schooling, different influences begin to play a more significant role. While parents still have a modelling role for many adolescents, it is friends, the peer group, siblings and the school which assume greater importance in the sports socialisation of the adolescent. How the following fifteen-year-old female was introduced to boxing reflects the importance of the peer group to her at this stage of her development: "Some of my friends were in the boxing club, so I just went along with them. They got me to join and now I love it."

Peer group networking allowed the following fourteen-year-old male an introduction to surfing: "It was my best friend's sister really that got involved first, then my best friend and I just followed and now we love it." Another fifteen-year-old male told how "my cousin played rugby and he dragged me along". The second-level school can also play a key role in introducing the adolescent to new sports. The following quote from a fourteen-year-old male suggests the importance of both primary and second-level schooling in the sports socialisation process: "I started rugby when I came here; in national school it was all hurling."

There were often a number of agencies of socialisation which adolescents felt were significant in introducing them to sport. One fourteen-year-old male remarked how "my father was very interested in hurling and so was the national school principal". Another fifteen-year-old female commented how "a lot of my friends were playing camogie and the headmaster in the school encouraged us all to take up a sport". There are a number of potential ways an adolescent can be introduced to sport but a common theme which emerged from the interviews was that if the adolescent, having been introduced to a new sport, felt good at that sport, they were more likely to take it up, often at a competitive level.

Van Wersche (1997) describes the importance of generating this "success circle". A thirteen-year-old female recounted how "at the start of doing athletics, we were doing competitions at school. That's how I was introduced to it, I really felt I was good

at it . . . my sports teacher said I should join a club and I did."
This quote, on analysis, reflects some interesting points and
how the interaction of certain criteria may lead to an adolescent
being socialised into sport. Firstly, the school had the facilities
and the equipment to introduce this girl to athletics. Secondly,
she felt competent at this activity and thirdly she received encouragement from a significant other, namely her sports
teacher. As a result of these three push factors, she joined a
club. If any of these three ingredients had been missing, she
may have been less likely to have taken up athletics.

There are a number of key agencies, including parents, siblings, the school system and peer groups, that often determine
whether or not the adolescent is socialised into sport. As noted
earlier, the primary agency, particularly in the early years, is
the family. As the child approaches adolescence, school and
peer groups then assume greater importance in introducing the
adolescent into new sports. If the adolescent is to be socialised
into sport, it is critical that these agencies play their part. If
there is little influence towards sport through parental modelling, the school system then assumes a greater importance.
What would appear clear, however, is that if sport is not promoted by these agencies, then it is unlikely that sport and
physical activity will remain outside the mental map of the adolescent. The adolescent will then be less likely to become an
active sports participant.

PE Classes

When the child enters the education system, the school becomes a significant socialisation agent for the young person.
Functionally, it is through the physical education programme
that adolescents are taught to be physically active and/or involved in sporting activities. There is little dispute by writers
that the contents of physical education programmes are variable. Kirk and Tinning describe how

> the kinds of physical activities that make up physical educa-
> tion programmes are the resultants of a number of structural
> and practical forces, in particular tradition, conscious selec-

tion and planning and a range of pragmatic factors such as facilities, equipment and teacher expertise (1990, p. 7).

This section aims to examine what adolescents felt about their school's physical education classes.

The reality of the PE experience varied significantly in the opinions of the respondents who were interviewed. Some loved PE whilst others did their best to avoid any participation. The level of PE provision was variable from school to school and it was the perception by adolescents that the status of PE was low in the overall hierarchy of school subjects. The reasons which were offered for liking PE seem to suggest that the biggest attribute of PE in the view of most adolescents was as a cathartic break from academic subjects. The PE experience in their second-level school was in general considered better than in their primary school.

For about half of the adolescents interviewed, PE was their favourite subject. One fourteen-year-old female commented: "it is the only thing I really look forward to in school". Another fifteen-year-old male was similarly enthusiastic about his PE classes: "While I enjoy most school subjects, PE is by far my favourite class." Approximately a quarter of those interviewed had diametrically opposing views. Consider the lengths to which this fifteen-year-old female went to skip her PE classes: "To get out of PE classes, I had to think of some different excuse each week and get a note from my parents every week." Another fourteen-year-old female was of like mind: "If you pretend you're sick or bring in a note, you do not have to do it."

For those students who liked doing PE, there was considerable uniformity in their stated reasons. This seventeen-year-old female liked the freedom PE offered: "With the other subjects, you have to be sat down. With PE you can just get up and do it." Another seventeen–year-old female favoured PE over classroom work because "doing PE is better than sitting in class all day doing other things. You get better enjoyment out of doing sport." However, there was considerable divergence in the reasons given for not liking PE. For some it was hygiene issues. One fifteen-year-old female commented: "I hate sport, all that running and sweating, oh my God." Others found single classes of PE too much hassle: "You've only one class and by the time you went from the classroom to the PE hall and changed you were losing time . . . then if we were late going back, the other teachers would be giving out." For others, there were competence issues. The following is a quote from a girl whose view would have been representative of about 10 per cent of those interviewed: "I do not like PE, I am just no good at any sports."

There appeared to be a general consensus, however, that the second-level school experience was better than the primary school PE experience. One fourteen-year-old female commented: "All we did in fifth and sixth standard was Irish dancing in PE. PE isn't good at all in the primary, it's much better here." Another seventeen-year-old female remembered that "in primary, nothing was organised for us but we used to play tag. There used to be a basketball court there but it was very small and if you wanted to play basketball, you had to bring in your own basketball." For this fifteen-year-old female, her primary school experience was "we just went down to the hall and we sort of danced around for a while, it was really disorganised" whilst, when she came into second-level "it was much better". This girl felt that PE at her second-level school was more structured and, as a result, she was happier learning more sports skills.

The general impression given by the adolescents is that for them, PE is peripheral to the main function of the school. One seventeen-year-old female recounted her story which was typical of many of her friends when she said: "PE is available up to third year. It is optional in fifth year but nobody bothers to do it. We do our homework instead." Another fourteen-year-old male (who had no PE teacher in his school) said: "It is PE on our timetable but he doesn't do PE with us, he just tells us to go home." In another school, a sixteen-year-old female remarked that "higher level students have PE once a week and lower level have it twice a week". The implicit message being given to pupils in these schools is the relative unimportance of PE to the central aims of their schools.

There appears to be little uniformity in either the type or level of PE provision on offer to the adolescents. According to various adolescents, some had single classes whilst a few others had triple classes in transition year. PE was optional in some schools; in others it was compulsory. Some schools had no PE teacher, others had up to four PE teachers. Some schools had an afternoon devoted to sport whilst others had PE allocated to all of a particular year at the same time. There clearly appears to be little consistency as to the nature of the PE experience given to this group of adolescents in the school setting.

The PE experience currently offered to Irish adolescents, in the views of the data set of Irish adolescents who were interviewed, appears to be variable. PE programmes, provided through the education system, offer the main opportunity to influence physical activity and sports participation levels of adolescents. The state, through the PE programme, has the opportunity to educate adolescents to be physically active for their adult lives. Through experiential education, competence acquisition and education for lifelong leisure, PE can have a significant role to play. However, the reality for most of the adolescents interviewed is that the main perceived positive characteristic of PE (amongst those who wanted to do the subject) is a general cathartic release from the rigours of academic pursuits.

PE Teachers/Trainers/Coaches

Significant others can play an important socialisation role in developing the sporting interests of adolescents (Coakley, 1996; Smoll and Smith, 1996). Physical education teachers, trainers and coaches in particular would be expected to exert the greatest influence. This section aims to outline the views of adolescents on how they feel about physical education teachers, trainers and coaches.

There are a number of central themes that emerge from an analysis of the selected adolescents' views of the people who were leading their sporting activities. In their view, there are not enough coaches/trainers working with young people. Secondly, when coaches/trainers are working with young people, it is important to the adolescent just how the coach treats them. There is a strong sense of equality sought, with a strong expectation that all pupils would be treated equally. It is also important that the adolescent likes and respects the trainer/PE teacher. Thirdly, many of the adolescents claim to hold the view that a significant number of PE teachers tend to focus on their favourite sport and do not give the adolescent the opportunity to participate in a wide range of activities.

The adolescent is often dependent on the trainer/PE teacher to facilitate them in playing their preferred sport. It would appear that with the current restrictions due to insurance requirements, many adolescents might not have access to facilities without adult supervision. In many cases, the adolescents are only too keen to play but cannot access the facility. One fifteen-year-old male claimed: "We were always trying to get to play in the sports hall at lunch time, but most of the time we could get no one to supervise us." Equally, the adolescent may need to be guided in the skills of a particular sport. Many students expressed sentiments similar to this fourteen-year-old female: "I used to do Gaelic last year, but the teacher we had went away and they couldn't get anyone else to do it." One seventeen-year-old female athlete commented on how her coach was overworked: "Our coach tries really hard but he's trying to coach about twelve different events, he much prefers coaching my event [middle distance] but he just has no help. He does his best."

Most adolescents had positive comments to make about their PE teachers and coaches: "She is really nice. She gives up a lot of time, every lunch time, she does hockey. She does it after school . . . it's great of her to give up her time."

Many students gave examples of the kind of commitment shown by coaches. One fourteen-year-old girl described how their Gaelic football coach literally rounded up his squad: "He came around twice a week and packed twelve of us into a Hiace van, he then drove us ten miles to training and dropped us home again. He had to bring us because there were not enough girls in his parish for a team." It would appear that some adolescents are dependent on the goodwill of their trainers/coaches for their sporting experience.

It is the norm for adolescents to have a strong sense of justice and to like all students to be treated equally. This point cropped up on many occasions in the interviews. A popular PE teacher was described in the following manner: "She acts the same to everyone. She treats us all fair." One fourteen-year-old male expressed a similar sentiment: "He treats everyone the same, he doesn't pick on anyone." However, some students felt the opposite about their PE teacher: "He has his favourites, gives them whatever they decide." Similarly, one seventeen-year-old female commented in relation to her PE teacher: "I hate her, she has all her own pets." Interestingly, only a handful commented on the coaching proficiency of their coach or PE teacher. The adolescents appeared more interested in the social skills and their interaction with their coach than in their coach's ability to impart skills. Perhaps the issue is that for many adolescents, the social aspect is more important to them than the actual sport or activity. One PE teacher reflected the view that "the activity is by and large irrelevant. They need attention and they like fun and social activities." Thus, PE programmes that over-emphasise games and skills teaching may not be of intrinsic interest to a significant percentage of adolescents.

A common gripe expressed by several of the adolescents was that PE classes appeared to them to reflect the interests of the particular PE teacher. One sixteen-year-old male said: "The PE teacher would always rather that we played rugby cause he was in the IRFU." Another pupil perceived that "all we ever did in PE was basketball", whilst a fifteen-year-old male who wanted to play soccer noted: "All we ever played was GAA outside and basketball inside, that's all the teacher liked to do." A sixteen-year-old male gave up PE because "all the teacher ever wanted to do was football, soccer and rugby and I was useless at those types of sport so I just gave up". Whilst these adolescents may be simplifying the school PE situation, as there may be many outside determinants affecting what the PE teacher can offer, many adolescents claimed that they liked to be involved in the decision as to what they did in their PE classes. The types of activities that they mentioned when they talked about PE also appear to confirm the fact that team games dominate the PE curriculum. This apparent over-emphasis on team games may be alienating a considerable number of adolescents and their dislike of team games may be a core reason for their non-participation in any type of sporting activity.

The role model of the PE teacher and/or trainer/coach is an important influence in the possible development of the sporting patterns of the adolescent. This relationship can be positive and may encourage participation, but equally a negative relationship may discourage the adolescent. The issue of the relationship seems to be more critical than the activity offered. A key question that this raises is: how does the coach's training address the issue of soft skills among coaches/trainers? It would appear that the imparting of these skills often comes as an afterthought compared to the emphasis on imparting the ability to teach skills. A fundamental rethink may be necessary if the views of the adolescents interviewed for this research are replicated throughout the country. Coaching and national governing bodies of sport may need to focus on the soft skills such as interpersonal skills, social and communication skills and to emphasise these skills equally with sports skills teaching. By doing this, they may, through an increased awareness of the importance of positive social interaction with adolescents, help keep more adolescents physically active.

Role Models

The final area examined in this section is the views of the adolescents in relation to role models. The fanatical interest displayed by adolescents towards certain musical bands is one example of the potential influence of role models on the adolescent lifestyle. Role models have been shown by writers like Epstein (1998) to be particularly influential in the teenage years.

There were several sporting role models who were admired by the adolescents who were interviewed. The role models were, in general, people connected with the main sport or activity pursued by the adolescent. Some international stars clearly had broad appeal for many adolescents. There were also some localised sporting heroes. These tended to be drawn from the ranks of GAA stars and from amongst these players adolescents tended to go for their local as opposed to national favourite. There would appear to be little doubt that extensive media coverage has significantly affected the participation patterns of Irish adolescents in sport, particularly soccer. Since the extensive coverage given to Jack Charlton's successful Irish soccer team and the advent of Sky Television, the numbers playing soccer in the schoolboy leagues in Ireland have doubled in the period from 1990 to 1998.

With the extensive coverage given to soccer, it is hardly surprising that the overwhelming majority of favourite stars or role models were soccer players playing in the English Premiership. Manchester United players dominated the popularity stakes. This appears to confirm the results of a study of schools in Dublin, which showed that the favourite team of over 50 per cent of primary school students was Manchester United. In relation to soccer stars, it was interesting to note that in the Premier league, English and foreign players were more popular with adolescents than the Irish players playing in England. Teenagers sometimes displayed an almost fanatical support for their favourite team and heroes. Interestingly, many adolescents supported English Premier league teams but had little interest in the Irish soccer leagues. There was also evidence of teenagers following different teams in different leagues and for different sports. One fifteen-year-old male said that he "supported Liverpool for ages, supported AC Milan in the Serie A and always supported Wexford (hurlers) during the summer". The fact that Waterford adolescents support English and Italian teams would appear to reflect the globalising effect of television as documented by writers such as Epstein (1998) and O'Toole (1997).

There were strong geographical differences amongst the GAA stars that the adolescents supported. While there was national respect for players such as D.J. Carey in hurling, the adolescents tended to be parochial in their choice of favourite role models in hurling or football. Local GAA stars got significant coverage in the local and regional media and there was often a feeling of them being "one of our own". A flavour of this is caught in this quote from one fourteen-year-old adolescent who talked about Waterford county hurler Tony Browne: "He taught us on our hurling summer camp, he's brilliant." Many adolescents said that they were often motivated to try and do their best by watching their role model in action. One fifteen-year-old male said: "When you watch the Man. United players on television, you'd like to be the same as them." One thirteen-year-old athlete admired Sonia O'Sullivan and said that she would "give you more reasons to work harder . . . you'd like to do as well as her".

Girls, in general, appeared to have a wider range of role models from a greater variety of sports than boys. One sixteen-year-old female athlete, for example, was a fan of Olympic hurdler Susan Smith and it helped that "she is from the same area as me and she went to the same school. I'd love to be like her." The blanket coverage given to soccer also attracted many female supporters. Just like the boys, many of the same group of current soccer stars were heroes to girls as well. "Giggsy", Owen, Keane and Beckham all figured highly in the popularity stakes. There were, however, several tongue-in-cheek comments regarding other assets of male sports athletes that some girls liked. One fourteen-year-old female liked André Agassi, whom she described as "a brilliant tennis player and good looking as well". Jason Sherlock was described as "handsome" whilst David Beckham was described as "gorgeous".

A small number of girls were unhappy about the scant coverage given to minority sports by the media. One fifteen-year-old female described how she had no real role model in her sport because they got so little coverage: "I do not know any hockey players because there is not much about them in the papers." Such lack of coverage is a major hindrance to the development of minority sports like hockey in Ireland. Another girl, who was still active in ballet at seventeen, said that while she had always been attracted to ballet, it was only through books and going to live performances that she maintained her interest and that ballet was hardly ever on television. She described how she was initially attracted to ballet: "I read the ballerina books . . . when you are reading those, you'd be living in a fantasy world where you would be going off to Russia and becoming a famous ballerina." She had experienced Russian ballets by going to several of their performances over the years and this had helped maintain her interest in ballet.

One interesting point of note was that there was little admiration for Ireland's first triple gold medallist, Michelle Smith. This probably reflects young people's disquiet over her later ban for taking performance-enhancing drugs. Or it may fit in with some sports feminist theories (Cahn, 1994; Hargreaves, 1994) that female sports personalities were portrayed as flawed heroines. Michelle Smith certainly had her share of detractors and there were several allegations of her using illegal sports performance-enhancing drugs in the aftermath of the Atlanta Olympics. Swimming is also not perceived as a popular sport in the eyes of the Irish public. In any event, the political and public reception she received paled into insignificance compared to the widespread adulation afforded to the Irish soccer team in 1990 and 1994 after their endeavours in the World Cups.

The media would appear to be a highly influential force among adolescents. Their behaviour, expectations and sports participation will often be influenced by how the media portray sports and sporting heroes. The changing behaviour on tennis courts is often attributed to the behaviour of John McEnroe during his heyday. Similarly, Eric Cantona's Kung Fu attack on a Crystal Palace supporter in 1997 was criticised by the judge in his prosecution because of the way he was regarded as a role model by adolescents. There would appear to be a masculinisation of sport as it is presented on television. As a result, many girls may only be aware of the sporting talents of male athletes. While the coverage for women's sports has increased in recent years, this could reasonably be argued to be a root cause for the lower rates of participation in sports amongst females in general.

Having examined the factors that influence the socialisation into sport and physical activity, the next section will examine the factors that encourage either continued participation (drivers) or drop-out (constraints) from sport and physical activity.

DRIVERS AND CONSTRAINTS TO PARTICIPATION IN SPORT AND PHYSICAL ACTIVITY

Any attempt to promote higher participation rates by adolescents in sport and physical activity needs to tackle this task from two sides. Firstly, by understanding the factors which encourage participation, which can allow for the fostering of conditions that will increase participation levels. Secondly, by understanding and reducing the causes of drop-out from sport, which could help decrease attrition rates. This section explores with the adolescents many of the drivers and constraints for them to participation in sports and physical activity. These include, amongst others issues such as gender and sports participation, social class groupings, geographical location, cost and facilities.

Social Class Groupings and Sport

The link between socio-economic status, social class background and educational failure is well documented by writers such as Lynch (1989). The aim of this section of the analysis of interviews was to attempt to ascertain how social class groupings impacted on sports participation and attitudes to sports amongst a selection of Irish adolescents.

School sports are an important element of the process of socialisation into sports for many adolescents. However, it has been argued (Hendry et al., 1993; Lynch, 1989) that many adolescents, particularly those from the lower social class groupings, reject school and school sport because of the perceived middle-class ethos of schools. Similar research shows that middle-class schools appear to perpetuate a middle-class ethos. In some instances this is overt, whilst in others it appears covert. Teachers are, according to Lynch, "very much part of the property-less middle classes and may well have a specific class interest in maintaining aspects of the status quo" (1989, p. 123). These differences in social origins appear to aggravate cultural differences between teachers and working-lass students. One PE teacher described how when she first came to her school in the 1980s, "it was a really strong soccer area but there was no soccer in the school . . . they only had Gaelic teams". This teacher felt that, at this time, soccer was a more working-class game whilst the teachers' sporting backgrounds were primarily in Gaelic games. If this was the case, there was certainly an element of enculturation being practised in this school.

Students from higher social class groupings are, in general, positive about the school experience and about school sport. Consider this quote from a Leaving Certificate male student who attends a private school: "I really like school . . . I think most of the teachers are top class. There are a couple who are a bit weak but, in general, I would say they are excellent. My sister and I have been encouraged to make the most out of school and my parents are very keen on school."

However, it is a different story with the lower social class groupings, particularly with those students who would be considered to be from the underclass. One fourteen-year-old female described her feelings: "I hate school because I get killed [picked on] by the teachers."

Griffin, in analysing identity in adolescents, claimed that "for marginalised groups, the experience of exclusion and of not being part of the establishment is crucially significant" (1993c, p. 302). Another sixteen-year-old female felt unwanted in certain sports facilities. She felt it was because "of where we are from . . . people treat us differently". The findings from the interviews would appear to bear out early work by Luschen, who stated that

> the different social classes have a culture of their own. Their greatest emphasis is on achievement and thus the highest sports participation is found in the middle class. It is considerably less important in the lower class where routine responsibility is valued (1970, p. 56).

Middle-class adolescents were drawn more to individual sports and the lower social class grouping appeared to either reject school sport or to stick to team/social sports. The counter-school culture as displayed by lower social class groupings was documented by Willis (1981), whose view was that it was their very rejection of school which made them suitable for semi-skilled or manual work. If this were the case, this hypothesis would explain the lack of mobility from the lower social class groupings, the perpetuation of low participation rates in sports and an over-emphasis on team sports such as soccer.

There is an established link between high education levels and high levels of sports participation (Coakley, 1996; McPherson et al., 1989). Bearing this in mind, the demographic statistics for Waterford City make interesting reading. An analysis of the 1991 census, as documented in the Waterford City APC report, found that 35 per cent of the adult population left school by the age of fifteen (in some wards, this figure was over 50 per cent). Only seventeen per cent of the city's workforce had a third level qualification. Given the apparent prominence of the effects of social networking in determining sports behaviour, it would appear that the individual's use of sports facilities is related to their immediate personal communities, particularly the influence of their friends, family and relatives. Adolescents from the lower social class groupings are at a disadvantage and this is reflected in a number of ways. It was noticeable that adolescents from lower social class groupings were more parochial in their attitudes and were less likely than middle-class adolescents to travel to facilities outside of their immediate neighbourhoods. The following girl typified this attitude when she said that she "wouldn't go down and train for basketball with that girls' school, none of our girls get on with them".

Some of the working-class adolescents appeared almost territorial in a few of their comments. One fourteen-year-old girl told how she and her friends "sat on the wall on their estate and moved on when the boys came along". A youth worker in the West Dublin area of Neilstown described why there were three community centres (all with sports facilities) located within half a mile of each other and how "the three estates see themselves as three different and independent communities and do not really mix". When probed on this view and on the economic rationale of having one large centre as opposed to three small centres, he made the following point: "It's not that simple, they would kill each other and ultimately one estate would claim ownership of the centre, so in reality you would end up excluding two estates."

There would appear to be a barrier to the lower social class groupings using facilities outside the mental map of their environment. Sport centres may not figure at all in the mental maps of adolescents from the lower social class groupings simply because the facility, whilst it may be close, may be in an area about which little or nothing is known. Perceptually, the facility may not be within their frame of reference. An example in Waterford would be the Municipal Golf Course, located in Williamstown and within the city boundaries. Adolescents from the lower social class groupings did not appear to be aware of the presence of this facility, even those who lived in the presence of this facility, even those who lived in the immediate vicinity of the course.

The areas with the greatest number of social problems were described as the least popular to live in by the respondents. For instance, with one exception, one particular area was felt not to be a nice place to live in. The adolescents living there felt there was consistent trouble within the estate. One fourteen-year-old female commented that "you'd get killed walking around the roads there, it is dangerous". The area itself has 4,500 people in 800 houses; 95 per cent of all housing is rented from the City Council while unemployment averages around 45 per cent. Approximately eighteen per cent of houses in the area are headed by a lone parent. Figures from the local community project show that only ten people from the area entered third-level education in 1998, even though the estate is located close to the local Institute of Technology and over 25 per cent of the population of the area are aged between fifteen and twenty-nine years of age. There also appeared to be a hierarchy evident, with adolescents from neighbouring estates almost looking condescendingly at adolescents from this area.

Amongst the students, there seemed to an unofficial ranking about the perceived relationship of their area to other areas. Because some adolescents had a high level of social problems to deal with, many were drawn to the local youth centre. This was a particularly popular place for girls to hang out. One thirteen-year-old female described it as "a safe place to hang out". Another sixteen-year-old female described it as a "sanctuary", whilst a third fifteen-year-old female described it as "a second home". Many students did their homework and several spent every evening there. It would appear that certainly for a number of adolescents, the centre was fulfilling certain needs that may not have been met at home. Many of these adolescents appeared to crave attention and as one PE teacher remarked: "The girls loved to do anything after school, all they wanted was a bit of attention and sadly, in a lot of instances, they did not want to face going home."

The institution of the school therefore appears to be fulfilling the sporting needs of the higher social class groupings in the main. It also appears to alienate many of the adolescents from the lower social class groupings. This role appears to be fulfilled in part for some adolescents by the youth centres, but some schools appear unable to change their ethos to accommodate adolescents from lower social class groupings. It is also critical that facilities are provided in the immediate vicinity of adolescents from lower social class groupings. Their mental maps appear to be tied into a specific local community and they may not be aware of facilities in nearby areas. Similarly, they may not be welcome or may not feel welcome there or it may not be safe for them to use facilities in other locations. It appears that a sporting ethos still permeates the higher social class groupings and is often alien to the lifestyle of the lower social class groupings.

Gender and Sport

The findings from the earlier statistical analysis carried out in this research show that sport is more associated with boys than girls. This section attempts to examine gender issues and see how these impact on sports participation. In particular, the reasons why more males are attracted to sport are examined as well as the factors which make some girls interested in sport. What appears clear is that there are agents of socialisation and cultural factors that predispose and encourage boys more so than girls to sports participation. Parents and significant others appear to be more encouraging to boys to be physically active while cultural factors appear to maintain homophobic and stereotypical attitudes as to the suitability of sports for different genders by many adolescents.

In general, parents appear more protective of girls than of boys. Girls frequently talked about their brothers being given greater latitude to pursue their sporting interests. One fourteen-year-old female stated that "my brothers always got it easier than me", whilst another fourteen-year-old female commented that "my parents never leave me out alone but my twelve-year-old brother can do what he likes". This may be a contributing factor to the reason that girls appear much more likely than boys to engage in activities based in the home. In general, girls appeared to do more homework, as was also found by Watson (1990b), listen to more music, watch more soaps on television and read more magazines. Girls also were expected to engage in household chores and in shopping (particularly on Saturdays with their mother), whilst these were not issues for boys. Adolescent boys were much more likely to engage in casual outside activities such as playing soccer on the local green. Girls also appeared to be allowed and encouraged to join structured leisure, e.g. after-school activities or the local youth centres. Boys, on the other hand, whilst they did join clubs, also appeared to engage in significant amounts of unstructured leisure in such activities as fishing, shooting some basketball, kicking about a football and roller skating. There is the added difficulty for girls that some parents did not want their daughters to play contact sports. One fourteen-year-old female told how "my parents do not like me to play camogie in case I get a bang or something".

Girls' experiences of how their sporting needs were catered for in primary school as compared to boys appear to have been mixed. Some girls claimed to have experienced equality, whilst others appeared to have had less sporting opportunities. One fifteen-year-old girl told how "we got to play [Gaelic football] in the Bord Na Scoil final three years ago. The rules had to be changed for us to play." However, she further added that "we played against the boys every day in our own school". This is in sharp contrast to the experiences of the seventeen-year-old female who said that "the boys were inclined to do sport whereas the girls did knitting and reading" and she seemed accepting of this hegemonic situation when she said "that is just the way it was I suppose". When girls were introduced to traditional male sports such as football and soccer, it was sometimes logistically difficult to carry on this interest as they moved through their teenage years. One fourteen-year-old girl who trained with the local boys in Gaelic commented that "as the only girl, I have to come already changed and I use another dressing room after training". Another sixteen-year-old female commented that "there is only one senior girls' football (soccer) team in the area and you have to be really good to get on it . . . girls aren't really catered for".

There seemed, in general, to be less provision for girls' as opposed to boys' sports. Girls who played camogie, football or soccer frequently complained that they were "second-class citizens", compared to the boys. One seventeen-year-old female told how her football team "had to call off a game because the lads wanted the pitch for training". Many of the camogie grounds pale into significance when compared to the hurling grounds. Some girls complained that "the dressing rooms were often shabby" or that "the grass was seldom cut". There was a general feeling that girls' sports came a poor second to boys' sports and the image of "girls sitting on the sidelines and watching boys play", as documented by Leaman (1984), often appears to be still the case. Not surprisingly, the reality is that girls are more likely to drop out of these team sports over the longer term.

Girls appeared particularly keen to have a friend to go along with them to their activity. One fifteen-year-old girl, when talking about her horse-riding pal, said that "it was nice to have someone to talk to about your interest as well as doing it with them". Other girls appeared reluctant to take up a new hobby if they had no one to go with. One seventeen-year-old female commented that "there is a rowing club that I would like to join, but I can't get anyone to go with me . . . they'd all know each other and I'd feel stupid sitting around". More girls than boys claimed to enjoy the recreational and social side of sports better. Many enjoyed the occasional recreational swim and significant numbers appeared to like to go walking with their friends or often with their mother.

There appeared to be a clear power differential between the genders in terms of their access to usage of sports facilities. There seemed to be an acceptance from girls that sports facilities were either primarily or even exclusively for boys. One fifteen-year-old female commented that "there is a soccer pitch down the road where the boys play, that's all there is". Another girl, in a co-educational school, said how there was "a pitch for hurling and football and for whatever the lads wanted to play". A teacher commented on how the boys would take over and dominate facilities if left to their own devices. She said how she started a badminton club before school as the country buses came in early. She had expected that the club would run itself but soon found that "if she did not set up a roster for games, the girls never got on". Another PE teacher commented on how "the boys always hog the hard court areas".

The observation of the use of play areas in schools by boys and girls indicated that boys appeared to dominate the courts, usually playing soccer, and girls looked on or went for walks. Some girls even described this as being the case in some PE classes. One sixteen-year-old female described her PE experience the previous year: "You could sit down and have a chat or she [PE teacher] might let us go for a stroll around the grounds or along the road . . . the lads usually played soccer and they'd want the full length of the gym anyway so that usually kicked the girls out of the gym unless they went upstairs. There was an upstairs where you could play badminton but that did not happen all that often." An interesting observation here is that in this situation, a female PE teacher appeared to be allowing greater priority to boys' sports.

An important theme that emerged from the interviews was that there certainly appeared to be gender stereotyping in relation to certain sports. Boys appeared more rigid in their views of what constituted male-appropriate sports. Males generally identified activities such as aerobics, gymnastics and Irish dancing as predominately female activities. In relation to aerobics, an eighteen-year-old male was of the view that "boys shouldn't do it, it wouldn't feel right. It's more of a woman's thing." There was often an underlying homophobic hint in the views expressed. One fifteen-year-old male, however, was more direct in his views on Irish dancing: "It is OK for boys . . . if they are gay." Boys in general gave more stereotypical views whilst about half the girls were liberal in their views with another half holding more traditional and stereotypical views. Girls were split in their views of the appropriateness of aerobics and Irish dancing for boys but interestingly almost all thought gymnastics was an appropriate activity for boys. Many saw no reason why males shouldn't take part in Irish dancing, for example. One thirteen-year-old female commented that "boys should do Irish dancing, everyone can dance". On the other hand, one fifteen-year-old female was of the view that "boys shouldn't do Irish dancing, they look like ponces". Homophobic views are prevalent in the views of many of the adolescents who were interviewed. Interestingly, a number of recent films including *Billy Elliot* and *Bend it like Beckham* have addressed these issues.

There were also some interesting views expressed in relation to girls participating in traditionally male sports. In relation to Gaelic football and soccer, a higher percentage of boys than girls viewed these sports as appropriate for girls. Boys, however, generally viewed both rugby and boxing as being out of bounds for girls whilst over a third of girls saw these as appropriate. Rugby was, in the opinion of one fifteen-year-old male, "too rough for girls". Another fourteen-year-old male thought that participating in rugby could take away from a girl's femininity: "Girls shouldn't play rugby because they would end up having big muscles and all that . . . they wouldn't look like girls." Many girls also felt that boxing was not appropriate for their gender: "Girls shouldn't box, they'd get hurt too easily." Others liked the self-defence benefits which could be attained by participating in sports such as boxing: "Boxing would help to toughen up girls so that they wouldn't be picked on by the boys."

The socialisation process appears to promote the suitability of sports for boys and to a lesser extent for girls. Girls appear to face greater obstacles and to receive less encouragement to pursue sporting interests. What is particularly worrying is that girls' interests appear to come second even within the school environment. While certain issues like allowing girls to wear trousers as part of their uniform has eased their ability to take part in school-ground sports in mixed schools, the overall needs of girls do not appear to be fulfilled, particularly in the mixed-school environment. Facilities and sports access appears much better for boys than girls. Strong infrastructural back-up is therefore needed to help increase girls' opportunities for sports participation. Similarly, a strong educational programme could possibly help both to banish some of the stereotypical and homophobic myths about the nature of sport and to promote its suitability for both genders. There certainly appears to be a strong case for a targeting of resources through positive discrimination to girls' sports in order to offer true equality of opportunity for all students, particularly in working-class areas.

Withdrawal from Sports and Disliked Aspects of Sport

The reasons given by students for giving up or disliking sport were many and varied. Nevertheless, there are a number of key factors that appear to be of particular significance as to why adolescents give up sport. These include injury of some sort, a perceived difficulty in participating, failure to make a team, finding the game too rough, the physical nature of the sport, an over-emphasis on competition, and other areas of their life assuming greater importance.

An injury or illness impacted in a number of ways. Asthma appears to be the primary medical condition which most impacts on adolescents. One fifteen-year-old girl found that her illness stifled her: "I have asthma and it is hard to keep running because I get out of breath a lot." The increasing prevalence of asthma would appear to pose particular problems amongst adolescents. Research by Flanagan (2002) shows that an estimated one in seven Irish adolescents now suffers from asthma. Injuries caused by various traumas also affected adolescents. A broken nose resulted in a thirteen-year-old girl giving up camogie: "My sister was playing camogie and she got a broken nose. She had a scar from that and decided to give it up." This particular girl's situation was exacerbated by her mother's disapproval of her playing camogie. The following comment from a sixteen-year-old male reflects the sentiment of many who would still like to play sport: "I used to play sports a lot but I can't anymore, I have a knee injury."

Withdrawal could also be linked to a number of context-related and logistical problems. A number of adolescents appeared keen to take part in sports but transport problems make participation difficult for them and, as a result, they often give up an activity. One girl who was commuting from the country to a city school said: "Most of the sports are after school, I can't do them because they are after school and my lift home would be gone." Another girl from Dublin commented: "I gave up swimming because I used to do it with the school but it was too difficult to get home. I had to get two buses home and that was with my hair wet, so I was always getting colds."

Getting a game in team sports would appear to be an important determinant of continued participation by the adolescent. They do not appear to be interested in sitting on the bench. A sixteen-year-old male said: "I used to go training all the time, they told us anyone who went training would be on the team but I was never good enough to get on the team, not even the B team, so I gave it up." Similarly a seventeen-year-old girl commented about her hockey experience: "It was great at the start, but towards the end of second year, it was all the A and the B team and there was no room for anyone else." It would certainly appear that there is often a greater demand for team sports than is currently being provided for in some schools. A PE teacher commented: "we had 64 students for first-year soccer trials, it was chaotic with only about fifteen places on offer and as a result we had a lot of disappointed students". Another PE teacher got around this dilemma by having a policy of fielding several teams. He felt that the girls were just interested in playing and being part of a team: "We had four cadet [first year] girls' basketball teams and there was no apparent stigma for the girls who played on the fourth team. Their match was just as important to them as a first team match." This reinforces a particularly important point. Adolescents want to play primarily for fun and they want to compete at their own level.

There were a number of adolescents who gave up sport because it was too rough for them. One fifteen-year-old girl commented: "We used to have basketball in primary. All the classes from first to sixth had PE at the same time. There were twenty against twenty on the basketball court so it used to be a vicious game. I gave up basketball because of that."

Whilst such a comment was more likely to come from girls, one fifteen-year-old male said: "I did boxing for three months. I gave it up, it was too rough for me." Another eighteen-year-old female recounted: "I took up camogie for a year but it was too rough, so I gave it up." Other adolescents disliked the way competition increased the physical nature of sport. One fourteen-year-old male commented how he "liked messing around with a soccer ball but disliked matches because people get too aggressive".

In adolescence, there are many competing interests for an adolescent's time and as a result sport often falls to the way-side. For some it was their social interests: "Soccer matches were on Saturday mornings and we'd be out all Friday night so I missed a few matches. They then started hassling me so I just gave up."

Others had jobs: "I was working twenty hours a week in a su-permarket, I did not have time for sport." This was a constraint that was impacting strongly in certain parts of Dublin. A camogie administrator described how "difficult it was to field a team at eleven o'clock on a Sunday morning because young people were either going to work or were so exhausted from working the night before . . . I knew that the clubs in Tallaght couldn't field teams on Sundays for six weeks before Christmas because their players were all working in The Square shopping centre."

Many other students gave their academic pursuits prefer-ence over their sports: "I gave up basketball because I had to study for the Leaving." This type of remark would have been a frequent and typical response from many students. These ado-lescents would appear to substantiate the claim by McPherson et al. (1989) that, in adolescence, there is a shift in the relative importance of sport with other age-appropriate activities.

Several other reasons, while not as frequent, were men-tioned in relation to early withdrawal from sports participation. It would appear that a change of teacher or coach could often lead to a number of students withdrawing from sport. A sixteen-year-old female commented: "I gave up tap-dancing because my teacher changed and my new teacher was dozy." Another reason that occasionally cropped up in the interviews was a feeling of being unwelcome. One seventeen-year-old female commented in relation to her tennis club: "It is not that you wouldn't get a game but you would feel very uncomfortable . . . the people that were in the tennis club were very snobby." A reason which appeared in a number of the girls' interviews was the problem of not having anyone to go with: "I used to play camogie but the girl I was going with was a bit younger than me so I was moved to a higher age group and there was no one there that I really knew, so I stopped going." Another fifteen-year-old female briefly gave up horse riding until a new facility opened: "I just did not like the place I was going to but when a new place opened, I went there." Interestingly, in this case the girl's liking of the activity was overshadowed by her dislike of the first facility she had been using.

It would thus appear that there are a plethora of reasons why particular individuals dislike or give up a particular sport or indeed drop out of sport altogether. From all of this, one thing at least is clear. Keeping adolescents involved in sport is a key area that needs to be tackled by any party interested in the promotion of youth sport. Once they leave, their likelihood of taking up sport again is reduced. Understanding and tackling the reasons for withdrawal from or disliking sports by adolescents is of fundamental importance to maintaining high levels of participation by this key group.

The Effect of Geographical Location on Sports Participation

This section examined the effects of living in a rural setting on participation in sport and physical activity. Adolescents from rural settings were questioned in relation to their access to sports facilities and organised physical activity, their sporting/leisure and lifestyle patterns, the closeness of other children for them to participate with and transport issues that might affect their physical activity patterns. An analysis of the views expressed by the rural respondents who were interviewed suggests that there are both positive and negative benefits to living in the country in relation to active sports participation. Some of the advantages include greater freedom to play, available facilities were often free and there was often a strong affinity with traditional Irish sports. The disadvantages included time constraints due to issues like long travel time to school, lack of transport to town or urban facilities and a restricted range of sports, the last factor often being further accentuated by a lack of trainers/coaches.

In general, rural children claimed that they were happy to be living in the country. A fourteen-year-old female commented: "I love the freedom and you know everyone"; whilst a sixteen-year-old male said: "The peace and quiet is lovely, it's healthy, it's safe." Because community and family links appear to be stronger in rural areas and added to the fact that living in rural Ireland is perceived to be safe, rural adolescents appear to be allowed greater freedom and many appear to spend more time outdoors. One seventeen-year-old male commented: "We are always out in the fields playing or down at the river fishing." Another fifteen-year-old female felt that she had more freedom than her town friends: "All my friends who live in the town say that it's boring and they are never let out and are stuck in their houses."

There would also appear to be a strong tradition of, and loyalty to, certain sports amongst the active rural adolescents. This is particularly noted in some of the views towards Gaelic games: "It is really a tradition down here, everyone plays Gaelic." This sentiment is echoed by a sixteen-year-old male: "My father is a football coach and my brother and I have always gone, it's like second nature to us." Interestingly, an eighteen-year-old Dublin adolescent also felt that Gaelic games were part of the rural subculture when he commented that: "I used to play a bit of Gaelic games in PE but I have never been very interested — I think it is a game played more by country people." Perhaps this is one of the reasons that the GAA only attracts 5 per cent of the metropolitan population to their sports (GAA Strategy, 2002). The rural adolescents also appear to have free or relatively cheap access to their local facilities. One fourteen-year-old male commented that "the local field [hurling] is always open and we can use it whenever we want". Another fourteen-year-old female was of the view that "you have to pay for everything in town whereas everything in our village is free".

There are, on the other hand, a number of disadvantages that were expressed by the rural respondents. A critical difficulty was the length of the school day due to having to catch buses: "We have to catch a bus early in the morning. It comes at eight o'clock and we are in school by twenty-past eight. Similarly, we are not home till five in the evening. That's a bit of a drag, especially in the winter when the nights are dark."

There were other transport issues which were frequently mentioned. The adolescents often had to be brought by car to their various activities. One fourteen-year-old female commented: "Mammy gives out because she sometimes has to drop us in and out of town [round trip of ten miles] three times a day." A sixteen-year-old male similarly echoed this view: "It is a hassle for our parents to drive us everywhere." One seventeen-year-old recounted how she gave up a chance to play competitive basketball with a club because of transport difficulties: "I live in a rural area. I got trials with the basketball team but transport in and out is virtually impossible so I couldn't go."

There would appear to be a consensus that there is a general lack of facilities, teams and coaches for country adolescents. One fourteen-year-old female said: "We only play basketball for the school as we haven't enough players in the community for a team." A seventeen-year-old male wanted a local facility: "There is nothing to do, we need a youth club"; whilst a sixteen-year-old camogie player asserted that "for the younger ones there are no trainers". This was a point that was also mentioned by many of the coaches. One coach commented that he had "noticed a severe depletion in the number of coaches particularly with rural [GAA] clubs".

It could be argued that the motivations for participation in sport and physical activity by country adolescents are driven more by context or personal reasons than their urban counterparts. As a result, physical activity provision appears to be more hit-or-miss in rural areas with less standardised provision than in Irish towns or cities. The PE programme takes on an additional significance for rural adolescents. This subject could allow the rural adolescents exposure to a variety of physical activities and to also educate them in the physical domain. It would appear that if they are not being catered for in the school setting, they could be easily disadvantaged outside of school. There is a strong likelihood that there will be a local GAA club in their locality, but that will generally be their only sporting opportunity. Exposure to a varied PE programme could compensate rural adolescents, thus allowing more of them the opportunity to experience a variety of lifelong sports.

Facilities

The availability and access to facilities has been cited by many writers as a key determinant of participation in sport by the adolescent. Veal (1994, p. 129), in his analysis of spatial demand, introduced his "distance decay" model. His basic treatise was that the further people lived from a facility, the less likely they were to use it. His theory would obviously have ramifications for the adolescent living in the more remote areas. However, there are a number of other interesting views that were expressed by the adolescents interviewed in this research. There were a number of age-specific facility provision gaps experienced by certain groupings in the research. Another sentiment expressed by some adolescents living in rapidly developing urban hinterlands was that new, large-scale housing developments were having a marked effect on their leisure opportunities.

There was a wide and diverse range of opinions expressed by the adolescents in relation to their views on facility provision and access. For some adolescents, there were lots of facilities but not enough time to use them all. One fifteen-year-old female stated: "There is so much to do, but I just do not have time for everything." Others were happy with the availability of their school hall: "We have different clubs and coaches every day after school, if we want." A significant number used outside facilities or clubs, some as frequently as every day. One fifteen-year-old female commented: "I go to the youth centre every day . . . because my friends come here and there are a load of good things going on."

For other adolescents, there was an apparent shortage of facilities to cater for their needs. One fifteen-year-old female commented: "All the swimming pools are miles from me, except for one, an open pool, so I can't go there, it's freezing." This view is interesting when analysed because it reflects an important factor in relation to facilities that recurs throughout the interviews. There are in fact three private swimming pools within relatively easy access for this girl. However, for many adolescents, private facilities were often either not mentioned or not considered accessible to them. Thus, private golf clubs, tennis clubs and private leisure centres, while in theory being available to adolescents, were not considered to be available by the adolescents themselves. This has important ramifications because real demand as borne out by participation rates will be determined by perceived availability of the facility to the adolescent as opposed to claimed availability of the facility.

Within the range of available facilities, there would nevertheless appear to be gaps in the facility provision for particular niches or groupings during the adolescent years. The following sentiment expressed by a sixteen-year-old female reflects the stated views of many of her contemporaries: "There are a good few things for people younger, but nothing for people our age." Another sixteen-year-old male commented: "There are no discos for our age group." Similarly, a fifteen-year-old female stated: "We would like a youth club for our age group so that we could hang out." Being around the fifteen- to sixteen-year-age group appears to pose problems for some adolescents. They consider themselves to have outgrown youth clubs and they no longer want to be doing things with their parents. At the same time, they are too young to be globally accepted in what appears to them to be peer-appropriate activities like drinking and going to nightclubs.

The problem, particularly with catering for adolescents over sixteen, was one that was mentioned by several of the youth leaders. Few of the youth centres ran programmes for this age group. One youth leader expressed a view that was reiterated by many of his colleagues when he said: "We only take children from between four and sixteen. The Department of Education are forcing us into certain programmes because most of the funding available is targeted at programmes preventing early school leavers [up to sixteen years of age] and unfortunately older adolescents lose out."

Some other adults working with this age group noticed a sudden falling away in attendance by certain age groups. A youth club leader commented: "They are great when they are twelve or thirteen but then all of a sudden they seem to lose interest and stop coming." Adults, on the other hand, sometimes find this age group the most difficult to handle. While the following view is extreme, it does reflect a stated view that the fourteen to eighteen age group are considered the most difficult to work with. A manager of a community centre in a strong working-class area of Dublin commenting on his centre stated: "These centres were built initially to keep youths off the streets.

These age groups [fourteen to eighteen] are always looking for discos. However, no one wants to work with them. Their parents can't control them, their schools can't control them, the police can't control them: why should we?" Interestingly, the centre he manages offers programmes for almost every age group except older adolescents.

Another interesting view was expressed by a number of adolescents living in urban sprawl areas. A number of these expressed views that their access to recreational facilities had disimproved. One seventeen-year-old female commented: "There used to be fields behind that we used to play in but they are all developed now." Another student was unhappy with the potential for recreation in his estate: "The new estates instead of having a green area, they have trees and landscaping; we have no recreational areas." One clear result of the Celtic Tiger has been a reduction in the amount of green space for play in and around cities and towns.

The availability and perceived availability of suitable facilities is one crucial element in an overall package that allows for the maximum participation by the greatest numbers. There would appear to be a need to cater for the middle to late second-level school years. Management of certain facilities also need to make themselves more teen-friendly. They may claim to be available but this is not the reality for many of the students. On the positive side, the majority of students are reasonably happy with the availability of facilities in their area and this should allow adolescents the opportunity to participate if they so desire.

Perceived Positive Aspects of Sports

This section of the interviews sought to ascertain from adolescents the kinds of things they liked about sports. By having an understanding of these factors, it may be easier to build programmes that would attract a greater percentage of students to remain active in sport. There are many aspects of sport which appeal to adolescents. The range and diversity of sporting activities are matched by the equally wide-ranging reasons given by adolescents for liking sports. Among the positive aspects of sport which were pinpointed were included the excitement and thrill of playing; a feeling of being good at the activity; the health or therapeutic reasons; the fun element; and being able to do things with friends. There are also a wide variety of reasons why particular sports appeal to different adolescents, with the individual competence of the adolescent in that sport being of particular importance.

A large number of the active adolescents claimed to enjoy the exhilarating nature of sport. One fifteen-year-old female was passionate about horse riding because of "the thrill of going fast, the jumping and the sensations, it's brilliant". Another fifteen-year-old male canoeist described how "you can't beat the sensation of shooting a big weir in high water", whilst a third adolescent "just loved being energetic". The physical nature and excitement of their game attract many adolescents. One fifteen-year-old female preferred camogie "because it's a skilful and exciting game". Basketball attracted another sixteen-year-old female because "it is a powerful and exciting game". Males claimed to particularly enjoy the physical nature of their sport. One thirteen-year-old male commented that he liked hurling because "it is a fast game and it is a tough game". Another sixteen-year-old male liked rugby because "it is the most physical and you can take your aggression out on the pitch".

A small number of adolescents were keen on the health or therapeutic aspect sport held for them. One seventeen-year-old female described how she liked swimming "because I have asthma and swimming helps". Another seventeen-year-old male talked about the benefit of his sport to his mental health. He was "basically going around doing six hours of walking, hunting and fishing" and found this "therapeutic and my mind can go away and think of other things for a while". Other students, like this fourteen-year-old female, found that "study is a lot easier when you are doing sport". Another seventeen-year-old female found ballet "always calms me personally and I love doing it". The therapeutic benefits of sports involvement for adolescents is an area which is often overlooked but, for the above interviewees, it was the aspect of sport which appealed to them most.

The importance of being with their peers was also a significant reason given for liking sport. Many students made comments such as this one from a fourteen-year-old female: "I just
love playing basketball with my friends." Having a good time
was also important. One seventeen-year-old male told how "we
have great fun when we go away playing rugby matches". Another seventeen-year-old male talked about the social benefits
of sport from his primary school experience: "It was a small
primary school . . . it was full of sport. This made the school feel
homely and helped make us a close-knit community."

From amongst those who were positively disposed towards
sports, a number of strands of interest could be detected. For
example, there was the pragmatic or seemingly pragmatic
edge to some respondents' reasons for pursuing certain sports.
A small number of boys commented on the possible cash benefits of playing well enough to do so professionally. In a similar
vein, one fourteen-year-old male commented how sports-
related qualifications can help secure jobs. He liked doing lifesaving "because it will help my CV". For others, the purpose
was, at least at face value, more autonomy-focused. In one instance, a positive attitude towards participation had to do with
self-reliance. One fourteen-year-old male completed sailing
exams because: "I've done the first and second stage . . . when
I am finished, I will have enough information on boats to sail on
my own. That's what I really want to do."

Many adolescents appear highly focused and ambitious. A
percentage are just as focused on sporting endeavour as on
other aspects of their lives such as success at school. These
achievement-oriented students like to obtain certification from
national governing bodies of sport where it is available and are
motivated by such recognition.

Whilst there was a vast array of different sports favoured by
individual students, there were a number of key reasons which
recurred as to why the adolescents preferred one sport over
another. Competence was a key issue. Adolescents tended to
prefer the sport at which they felt they could perform well. One
fifteen-year-old female stated that "camogie is my favourite
sport, it is the one I'm best at". Another sixteen-year-old female
stuck to athletics "mainly because I was good at it". One seven-

teen-year-old female described why she went orienteering: "I love it and I'm good at it." This feeling was further reinforced by other adolescents when their achievements were rewarded: "I have always been good at sports and I have got lots of awards for playing". Others preferred team games because "I get to meet new people". At the other end of the continuum, a thirteen-year-old female sought solitude in her athletics: "I love being able to do it on my own and it gives me time to myself."

The diversity of reasons given for liking sport gives an indication of the perceived wide range of benefits that can be gained from participating in sport. It also gives an indication of the complex and differing egocentric interests and likes of adolescents. For this reason, it would appear important that the adolescent is given the opportunity to participate in, and become competent in, a wide variety of sports. An awareness of an individual adolescent's likes in sport should also help in the planning of individual programmes for adolescents. This concept, which is evidenced in programmes like The President's Award or The Duke of Edinburgh Award or an individual PE contract drawn up with the adolescent where each individual selects activities of their choice, would give the greatest chance of positive lifelong participation by each adolescent in sport of some form.

Time and Cost

Lack of time is often a reason cited for giving up leisure activities by adults (Hendry et al., 1993). This section sought to examine how much the sporting activities of adolescents were restricted by time constraints. The results found that adolescents were particularly restricted in the years in which they were studying for state examinations. However, there were also windows of opportunity for increasing participation rates in physical activities in years such as Transition Year, where the curriculum allowed more time and flexibility to introduce new and varying activities. The cost of taking part in sport and physical activities was also investigated. The adolescents' replies show that while cost is an issue for some adolescents, it does not appear to be a significant constraint to participation amongst the adolescents interviewed.

Adolescents are aware of time constraints, particularly in their national exam years. Comments like this, from a sixteen-year-old female, would be typical: "At the moment, I am in sixth year and I do not have time." Another seventeen-year-old male similarly commented that "I haven't time to play sports because of study, that is a priority." On the other hand, there were also some perceived opportunities for extra sports participation particularly during Transition Year. Practically all the adolescents who were interviewed regarded this as a "doss year" and one fifteen-year-old female saw it "as a year that I can really concentrate on my sports, to be good at them and to improve". In a similar vein, one sixteen-year-old male commented that "we're in Transition Year now so we're doing nothing for the year and we'll have plenty of time for sport." The Transition Year programme thus offers a real opportunity for schools to expose adolescents to a variety of lifelong sports.

While cost was occasionally mentioned as a barrier to the use of leisure facilities, this was in general the exception rather than the rule. However, the private leisure centres were considered too expensive to join. One fourteen-year-old female thought that "the pools in the hotel leisure centres were too expensive to use". Another seventeen-year-old male commented that "the leisure centre costs about €350 a year to be a member of the gym and then you have to have transport". Another girl found a private gym to be too expensive to use on a regular basis: "It is too dear when you go twice a week, it is €4 per session, so I only use it once a week". The cost of gear was occasionally mentioned as a hassle. One fourteen-year-old male, who played soccer, commented that "you have to pay €80 for a decent pair of boots and then you have to pay €20 for a pair of shorts . . . you also have to pay the club money for insurance." Another fourteen-year-old enjoyed canoeing but for her, "every time you go an instructor and boat costs between fifteen and twenty euros, it's so costly". There were some facilities which were occasionally mentioned which had not been visited or checked out as the adolescents felt that they were too expensive to even enquire into that possibility. One seventeen-year-old male thought that "the golfing scene was a bit too expensive to join". So even though he expressed a desire to try golf, he hadn't followed up his interest because he had just "presumed it was too expensive".

In general, adolescents claimed they were satisfied at the costs that facilities charged them. There seemed to be plenty of subsidised facilities available. One fifteen-year-old male told how "you can rent out the hall for 50 cents each". Whilst another fourteen-year-old female felt that her swimming was reasonably priced: "It is only a euro a go, so that is grand." Another seventeen-year-old female noted that "sport was not so costly in her school". There were also several subsidised trips available. One sixteen-year-old-female, who attended the local youth centre, commented that "weekend trips like we do in some other places would cost you €70, but we only have to pay €5". What appeared to come across from many of the interviews was that, time after time, adolescents were able to use personal contacts to gain cheap entry into facilities.

The family network appears to be strong for many of the adolescents who were interviewed and social networking appears to be widely practised. One fourteen-year-old female explained how she went swimming because her uncle worked there and she got in for free. Another fourteen-year-old female told how her aunt was a member of a leisure centre and she went with her sometimes. Several others had free or reduced access to sports facilities through their parents' social clubs. One sixteen-year-old female told how "we used to get free swimming when we went with Dad's work group". Waterford Crystal is the largest employer in Waterford with approximately 1,500 employees. They have their own leisure centre and families of workers have privileges there. One fifteen-year-old, whose father worked there, commented that she could "go swimming, do aerobics or play pitch and putt at the Glass centre". School sports halls appeared to be widely available and free to use for most students. One girl was involved three evenings a week "and it is all free". This type of provision by schools is often overlooked but its impact on adolescent sporting participation levels may be significant.

The issue of time for sports participation is one that is critical for adolescents, particularly during their exam years in second-level schooling. This issue is exacerbated because as well as the adolescents often perceiving that they do not have time to do sports with their study, many schools reduce, or eliminate altogether, PE provision during exam years. This ultimately may be one of the biggest contributors to long-term falling away from sports participation, as it is placing sport lower down the scale of priorities for many adolescents. If adolescents pull out for a year due to exams, it is probable that a percentage will not resume their participation. On the issue of cost, it appears important to encourage good sports participation that cheap, or at least reasonably priced, sporting facilities be widely available. There would appear to be a threshold of acceptable prices for the use of facilities by adolescents. In general, adolescents seem to be making good use of school and community-run leisure facilities. However, adolescents do not appear to be availing of private leisure centres to any great degree. The importance therefore of keeping, for example, school halls available in the afternoons would appear to be a critical point in encouraging and maintaining good sports participation levels by adolescents, a factor which may be currently overlooked.

LIFESTYLE CHARACTERISTICS OF IRISH ADOLESCENTS

There are a number of broad societal factors that the research confirms as major influences in the lives of many Irish adolescents. Changing economic needs have put a premium on staying on in school and moving on to third-level education. The mass media appear to be an omnipresent force in the lives of most teenagers. Many young people also appear to be able to afford and enjoy a lifestyle and a standard of living that would be significantly higher than that of their parents when they were teenagers. Thus many adolescents would have greater opportunities to travel, more access to money and to a more varied lifestyle. Adolescents often appear to display high levels of egocentricity (Hendry et al., 1993) and, as a result, their sporting, leisure and lifestyle patterns will often be dictated by putting their own interests first. They use this stage of their lives to try different lifestyles and leisure interests and also move to socialising with peers and adults outside the family. Similarly, the period of adolescence is often a psychologically challenging time for adolescents. As a result, much of their time is spent on activities that are hard to quantify. Some teenagers run up phone bills talking to their friends for hours. Similarly, a large amount of time may be spent "hanging out" or being alone. The interplay of these factors on the lifestyle patterns of some adolescents will now be explored. These areas are examined as the way in which they prioritise their lifestyle behaviour and patterns will dictate if there is a place for sport and physical activity within that lifestyle.

Leisure and Lifestyle Patterns of Adolescents

The Irish government appears to place education high on their list of priorities. Their strong belief in the value of education is demonstrated by their moving of the compulsory school leaving age from fifteen to sixteen in 1999, and in their stated aim that by the year 2000, 90 per cent of students would finish second-level education.[1] They are also increasing their financial investment in education at all levels. As a result, it is hardly surprising that school appears to be central to the lives of most of the adolescents who were interviewed. Apart from the actual time spent in school, the educational demands appear to consume considerable amounts of the adolescents' time. One thirteen-year-old found a considerable difference between first and second level: "When I moved into secondary school, I was amazed at the amount of homework we had to do." Indeed, there appeared to be several students who took part in supervised study. This was often in their own school: "We have supervised study for two hours Monday to Thursday in school and when I go home, I do between one and two more hours after supper." Supervised study was also availed of in many of the youth projects. One fourteen-year-old female commented: "We have a homework club every evening. It is much easier to study there than at home."

---

[1] Outlined in the Department of Education and Science White Paper, *Charting our Education Future*.

For many adolescents, their life consisted mainly of a cycle of school and study with little time left for other activities: "Now with school and study, all my pastimes are gone." It would seem from the attitude and comments conveyed in the interviews that girls would appear to be more diligent in their studies than boys. The time spent studying by girls varied on a continuum of one to five hours per night. They appeared to have a more serious attitude to their homework, whereas there was often a laddish view to school and to doing homework talked about by some boys, as exemplified by this fourteen-year-old male: "I never do homework, I've other things to be doing." However, this sixteen-year-old male appeared to accept that you had no realistic choice except to stay in school: "The way I see it, you have to go to school . . . I'll definitely go on to college." Others felt they had no other realistic options. This fifteen-year-old male was fatalistic in his view that "I do not want to go to college but I'll probably have to." The diligence of girls in doing their homework appears to confirm findings by Drummy and Watson (1992) that 73 per cent of girls spent more than 90 minutes on their homework compared to 30 per cent of the boys. The points pressure in Irish second-level schools and the amount of time taken up with study in order to achieve the necessary points for college is clearly displacing the amount of time available for sport for many adolescents.

Spending time socialising, chatting or just hanging out with their peers appeared to be a major element in the lifestyle of many of the adolescents interviewed. For many teenagers, this resulted in conflict over the length of time spent on the phone, particularly amongst girls. One thirteen-year-old female commented on how "my parents say that I spend far too long on the phone talking to my friends". Another fifteen-year-old female told how her sister "spent hours on the phone to her friends". A third fifteen-year-old female told how her boyfriend lives in Dublin and "we're always talking on the phone". Whether this is a real or fantasy world is difficult to ascertain but many teenage girls appear to model their lifestyle on their favourite characters from programmes such as *Home and Away* and this is the kind of lifestyle they like to claim to be living.

Hanging around appeared to a major lifestyle pattern of the adolescents interviewed. There were many forms of hanging around described. Some talked about "sitting on walls", others frequently "hung around at the local supermarket", whilst others mentioned "buzzing around".[2] It appeared that hanging around was an expected pattern of activity by the adolescents themselves. One fourteen-year-old female related that "we just hang around like normal teenagers". The "culture of the bedroom" (Frith, 1978) features prominently, particularly in the girls' interviews. This comment by a sixteen-year-old female appears to reflect the leisure patterns of many teenage girls: "When I go to my friends, we go up to her bedroom, we just sit and chat, listen to music and stuff." Another sixteen-year-old female related how "we do not really go into town much any more, we just stay in each other's bedrooms and have our own buzz". Occasionally, the hanging around led to deviant behaviour. One seventeen-year-old female told how "weekdays after school, I hang around with my friends on the street. For fun, we bang on a few doors and throw a few eggs at windows. The odd time as well we play tiff.[3] That's a laugh because we are in other people's gardens and we get chased." While this last comment represents the stereotypical attitude of many adults as to what happens when groups of teenagers hang around, it is worth emphasising that, for the vast majority, hanging around involves innocent fun or social activities.

The mass media seemed to play an important part in adolescent life. Watching television, listening to music and reading magazines appeared to be significant in many of the adolescents' lives. Television would appear to be particularly influential. The role of the television would appear to be pervasive for many adolescents. All but one of the adolescents interviewed had a television in their house. Many even had a television in their own room. Adolescents appear to watch the same pro-

---

[2] This was a colloquialism used particularly in Dublin which appeared to mean going around in a group looking for some excitement, e.g. roller blading.

[3] This was a colloquialism which appeared localised within certain working-class parts of Waterford — the function of this game appeared to be to annoy neighbours.

grammes as adults. Soaps appeared to be particularly popular, with many adolescents listing off several soaps that they watch regularly. Particularly popular were *Coronation Street*, *East-enders*, *Fair City*, *Dawson's Creek* and *Home and Away*. Comedies also appealed to teenagers. Particular favourites included *Friends*, *South Park* and *Father Ted*. As the vast majority of the adolescents interviewed watch primarily adult shows on television, it is no surprise that most of them aspire to an adult lifestyle.

There were gender differences in relation to attitudes to sports programmes. Many males were fanatical in watching sport on television whilst girls were in general much more ambivalent. One sixteen-year-old male watched soccer most nights and "generally whatever sport is on except golf". Practically all of the adolescents interviewed spend significant amounts of time watching television. This is also the main activity that they appear to do with their parents. A fifteen-year-old girl told how "I watch all the channels. We have the satellite dish and I never stop watching it every night." Another four-teen-year-old male told how joining a youth project changed his viewing habits, which were still considerable: "Before I used to watch television for more than five hours each day. Since I joined, I only watch it for three hours each day now." The youth centre has therefore been influential in partially changing the current lifestyle pattern of this adolescent.

As a result of awareness gained through watching television and reading magazines, it would appear that there is an apparent link between their awareness of products endorsed in the media and their spending patterns. Many adolescents are keen consumers of expensive designer casual clothes and of sports and music items. One coach was particularly annoyed about the loyalty of some adolescents to branded merchandise: "Some players will go out and spend €100 on football boots, not because they are good boots but because Ryan Giggs or Zola has these boots . . . it's crazy when you see kids from families that do not have much money with a really expensive pair of boots; it's pure madness."

Many adolescents only buy branded sports gear and many teenagers are able to reel off the names of their favourite designer clothes labels. These findings appear to replicate results outlined in "Behaviour and Attitudes of Teenagers", a survey carried out by the Institute of Advertising Practitioners in Ireland.[4] They found that Irish "teenagers are highly brand conscious and, even by the time they are thirteen years old, they have definite preferences. Adolescents thus appear to be a large niche group for marketing agencies and many companies are offering special incentives in an effort to generate lifelong custom. The main banks, for example, appear to have links in several schools and many students use their special accounts."

However some of the companies which really appear to be penetrating the adolescent market are the cigarette and drink companies. Smoking was prevalent amongst a large minority of adolescents. Some teenagers were covert about their smoking. One fifteen-year-old female told how she smoked but that "my mother would kill me if she found out". Others are smoking openly: "I chain smoke but my mother doesn't mind and my father has accepted it." Whilst it appears that smoking is not allowed in the school environment, this does not seem to deter some adolescents. One seventeen-year-old female related how she "went out to the back of the toilets every break for a fag". Interestingly, some of the non-smokers vehemently disliked smoking. One fourteen-year-old female said: "My mother smokes, I think it is horrible. I can't stand being around it." Accessing cigarettes did not appear to be a problem for the teenagers. They were most often bought in tens but many could also buy them singly. This is despite the fact that it is illegal for under-sixteens to buy cigarettes in Ireland.

If anything, alcohol consumption appears more widespread than smoking. There would appear to be a *normality* about drinking alcohol in the psyche of Irish adolescents from early on in second-level schooling. Most adolescents who were interviewed had tried drink and many claimed that they were regular drinkers. Many first years were already experimenting with alcohol. A number of thirteen-year-olds described drinking cider "across the road on the green". One sixteen-year-old male described how he "used to drink to get drunk but now just

---

[4] Findings summarised in *The Irish Times*, 16 September 1999.

drinks socially". Another fifteen-year-old female likes variety in her drinking: "I like Carling, Woodies [strawberry flavour], Bacardi and if I'm out for a good night out, I drink Black Russians, they blow the head off you."

By the time many adolescents reach sixteen to eighteen years of age, some like to think of themselves as seasoned drinkers. One eighteen-year-old male stated: "I'm trying to cut down a bit now, I do not drink as much as I used to." For others, drinking was an integral part of their normal socialising. One seventeen-year-old male described his normal weekend: "We'd usually go out on a Friday night to the pub for a few pints. Then we go to the [named venue]. Saturday night depends on if someone's got a free gaff [house] or not. We'd usually go to someone's house and have about seven or eight cans."

Accessing drink was described as problematic but the adolescents all seemed to manage to acquire drink. It appeared also that, even in small towns, there was usually at least one pub that served adolescents. One fourteen-year-old female, who was talking about a no-name disco,[5] told how "they do not allow alcoholic drink but we sneak it in anyway".

Increasingly, people working with youths appear to be attempting to highlight the issue of underage drinking. A principal in a Mayo school in a newspaper article in 2001 told how half his students were missing one Monday after a festival in the town the previous day. In a subsequent television interview, he attributed most of this absenteeism directly to drinking. Similarly, each year after the Junior Certificate results are released, there is a media outcry about the drinking behaviour and celebrations of fourteen- and fifteen-year-olds. Drinking would therefore appear to be endemic and a widely acceptable social activity amongst a significant number of those adolescents who were interviewed.

Another aspect that was evident from the interviews was that through their interests, hobbies or clubs, many adolescents had been afforded the opportunity to travel either within Ireland or abroad or both. One fifteen-year-old related some of the places

---

[5] "No-name discos" were set up in various parts of Ireland in an effort to provide drink-free settings for discos, mainly for the younger adolescents.

she had been to with the youth centre: "We've gone on several trips to the mountains, we went to an outdoor pursuits centre in Kinsale and last year we went on the bus to Spain." Another seventeen-year-old female talked about her activities with the Rangers: "They're like the Guides, we go off on trips . . . to places like Trabolgan, Wacky Warriors, weekends away." The widespread travel by adolescents appears to confirm results published by "Behaviour and Attitudes of Teenagers" (1999) which showed that almost eight in ten teenagers had travelled abroad at some stage and over half had travelled further than Britain.

One exceptional fourteen-year-old male had had been on several trials with soccer clubs in the United Kingdom. On the Monday of his interview, he related how he had been on a trial with Celtic the preceding weekend: "I flew over on Saturday and came back last night, they met me at the airport, gave me digs and €60 for the weekend." Another fourteen-year-old male, who was into greyhound racing with his father, told how "we go to all the race meetings right around the country". Many of the adolescents supported a sports team, often with their parents, and as a result travelled in support of them: "We follow the county team all over the country, everywhere they are playing." Another fourteen-year-old female travelled extensively with her marching band: "We go away all the time. Last year we went to England . . . we go to different competitions all over Ireland." Their particular schools often also offered the students many opportunities of travel. Different activities mentioned were trips to outdoor pursuits centres, French exchange trips, trips to cities for plays or shows, particularly in Transition Year, school tours to Europe, trips away to play games, trips to the Young Scientist Exhibition, visiting the Kellogg's PE Awards, trips to open days in colleges and universities, information technology outings and religious retreats. Many other adolescents had been to Spain or France with their parents on holidays or others had spent a month in the Gaeltacht or at week-long summer or sports camps. Most adolescents would appear to have reasonable opportunities to travel throughout their school years.

Another significant area that appeared to impact on many adolescents' lifestyles was work. Many of those questioned found the cost of living expensive and also did not like being dependent on their parents. They often realised, like this thirteen-year-old male, that their parents hadn't an endless reserve of money: "I'd like to work because you'd want things and you wouldn't want to be asking your mother everyday for money . . . you'd have her bankrupt." There appeared to be work available, particularly by the time adolescents were fifteen or sixteen years of age. One fifteen-year-old female told how "the local supermarket can give you work everyday and they open till 11 p.m. on Friday nights". Another sixteen-year-old female, who appeared to live an adult-type lifestyle as she smoked and drank and went to discos each weekend, earned in the region of €80 per week from "working four evenings a week and from 8.30 a.m. to 6.30 p.m. every Saturday in Roche's". Many adolescents aspired to being financially independent and to spending their money on the goods and services that they wanted.

Other adolescents were involved in voluntary work. Some helped out with the Special Olympics and others were involved in first aid or lifesaving organisations. Others were involved in voluntary projects either through Transition Year or doing the President's Award. One sixteen-year-old female who was doing her bronze award told how she "worked every Saturday in Barnardos, in their consignment shop". Some adolescents were involved in their family business and felt they had to help out there. Work was therefore impacting on the potential leisure time of many adolescents.

From the interviews carried out with adolescents, it would appear that several factors impact strongly on their lifestyle. School is particularly influential in their lives. Whether they like it or not, they have to attend school until they are sixteen and with academic qualification inflation, it is almost inevitable that many of them will of necessity end up in college. Education can afford many opportunities for the adolescent. For many, it prolongs their childhood and, unlike their parents, they will be entering the world of work at an older age. For many others, it increases their expectations from life and allows them to be socially mobile. One thirteen-year-old male felt that "school is important to get a good job. I do not want to be filthy all my life like my father who is a fitter." School also offers opportunities and education for adolescents in a variety of settings, whether this is through travel, the PE class, Transition Year, outside clubs and societies or even just the opportunity to hang around with their friends.

Adolescence may also be a time of exploring and a move away from the influence of parents as significant others to the prominent role of the peer group in their lives. Thus much of the adolescents' leisure time was involved in activities such as hanging around. Whilst it is difficult to quantify the exact nature of what they are doing when hanging around, it does appear to form a significant role in their lives and is seen to be normal teenager activity. Many young people also seem to benefit from improved living standards with increasing access to such accessories as mobile phones and televisions in their own room. Most expected to have their own room and had access to reasonable spending money. The majority of adolescents expected to be able to buy branded merchandise as the norm. Several had travelled quite a bit and socialising at least once a week was normal behaviour for most adolescents. Similarly, the drinking of alcohol would appear to be a widespread activity amongst adolescents.

Another area that appears to be impacting on adolescents is work. Many adolescents work to fund a lifestyle that is often comparable to adults. The money they earn independently allows them significant influence in pursuing their chosen leisure activities. Adolescents' leisure time therefore is a period of exploration and change when different lifestyles can be tried and exchanged. The adolescents, through their leisure activity or work, are allowed avenues where they can socialise with peers and adults outside of their immediate family. They are moving from childhood to adulthood at different rates. The changing and often adult-like lifestyle they live reflects this transition.

Chapter 10

KEY FINDINGS AND EMERGENT THEMES

This chapter serves two main purposes. Firstly, it provides an overview of the key findings from this research and places these findings in the context of international research. Secondly, this chapter proposes a number of emergent themes concerning the theoretical interpretations of the data that have emerged as a result of this research.

KEY FINDINGS

For the purposes of clarity, the key findings from this research are presented under a number of categories, namely, lifestyle issues, sport, school, gender and social class grouping issues.

Lifestyle Issues

The eleven key findings in relation to lifestyle issues are:

1. Watching television and other home-based leisure activities are the dominant leisure activities of adolescents.

2. Most adolescents claim to enjoy physical activity, but it may not be part of their lifestyle because of displacement by activities such as computer games and socialising.

3. There is a definite movement from organised to casual to commercial leisure activities as adolescents get older.

4. Youth groups are only popular amongst a small minority and these tend to be the younger adolescents.

5. Adolescents appear, in general, to be well travelled and many place a strong emphasis on their education.

6. Older adolescents express a clear desire to have an adult lifestyle.

7. Many adolescents appear to be individualistic and their leisure behaviour appears to be less determined by traditional links with family and school and more influenced by individual choice.

8. Hanging around with peers is a particularly popular leisure activity with adolescents.

9. A high percentage of adolescents claim to drink. Smoking is also a popular lifestyle activity for a significant percentage.

10. Over one-third of adolescents work part-time.

11. Physical activity/sport do not dominate the life experiences of adolescents.

Sport

The eight key findings in relation to sporting issues are:

1. The key ways that adolescents are socialised into sport include parents, peers and school.

2. A total of 27 per cent claimed not to take part in any sport.

3. Two-thirds of the sports participated in were outdoor sports.

4. Sports provision by schools and clubs is dominated by the traditional sports.

5. There would appear to be a clear lack of provision for non-first team players.

6. There is a marked decline in sporting and activity levels linked to age throughout adolescence. As adolescents get older, they drop away from sport and physical activity. Issues such as new interests and failure to make a team were key reasons for many adolescents dropping out of sport.

7. Many adolescents would like the opportunity to experience alternative sports which offer immediate enjoyment, relaxation and recreation opportunities.

8. The mass media are helping to promote the popularity of certain sports, particularly soccer.

School

The four key findings in relation to school issues are:

1. School provision is dominated by team sports.

2. Schools appear to over-emphasise the role of competitions and coaches.

3. There has been a movement towards the secularisation of education in recent years and this may affect the availability of sporting facilities in the coming years.

4. Physical education in Irish schools appears to be at a significant crossroads (crisis).

Gender Issues

The five key findings in relation to gender issues are:

1. Many boys are particularly active in outdoor sports whilst active girls are as likely to be involved in indoor as outdoor sports.

2. Adolescent males engage more in outdoor aggressive activities while females involve themselves more in indoor feminine activities.

3. There are greater opportunities for extracurricular sporting activities for boys in schools and clubs.

4. There are many areas where female and male youths agree. For instance, boys and girls both agree that having fun is the main reason to be physically active.

5. Girls are still not socialised into sports as much as males and particularly not into certain sports. However, there would appear to be a clear move towards the democratisation of participation between the sexes. Males are more active than females in team sports but the same disparity does not exist in individual sports.

Social Class Grouping Issues

The three key findings in relation to social class grouping issues are:

1. Social class grouping gives an indication of the likelihood of an individual participating in physical activity/sport and also of the activities in which they are likely to be active.

2. The higher an adolescent's social class grouping, the more likely they are to be physically active and in a greater variety of activities than an adolescent from a lower social class grouping.

3. For working-class students in particular, there appears to be a clear association of leisure pursuits with school discipline, which appears to alienate many pupils from school sport.

Overview of Key Findings

In the latter decades of the twentieth century, social conventions have given adolescents greater self-determination at increasingly younger ages and as a result, current social expectations for youth are particularly problematic. Added to this, there appears to be an increasing blurring of the distinction between adolescent and adult lifestyles and this transition is complicated by the fact that there are no longer any symbolic rites of passage from adolescence to adulthood. At age fifteen, for instance, adolescents cannot vote, they cannot smoke, drive or drink and, legally, they are still minors. However, the fact that some activities are illegal does not deter some adolescents. At this stage of their lives, many adolescents are engaging in what were traditionally adult activities. A percentage take part in (some or all) activities such as drinking and smoking, are sexually active and engage in drug taking. They are no longer children but they are not adults either.

In the last couple of decades in particular, the concept of youth culture has entered a new realm. The relatively distinct boundaries between the concepts of childhood, adolescence and adulthood have become unclear. For example, many adolescents have to make crucial decisions in their mid-teen years that may affect the rest of their lives. Questions arise, such as staying in or quitting school, entering the workforce, and, if they do stay in school, the subjects they select which may affect their future career path. The decision to engage in sport and/or physical activity is only one of many decisions made by each individual. The reality is that for a myriad of reasons many Irish adolescents are not involved in sport and/or physical activity and the percentage of those who do not take part increases as they progress through adolescence. Irish teenagers appear to have one of the poorest levels of physical activity in the European Union, with a study by Watson (2000) claiming that Irish adolescents are the "greatest couch potatoes in Europe".

The relatively low prioritisation given to sports by many adolescents appears to be a worldwide issue. Kirshnit, Ham and Richards (1989) in the US found that only a very small portion (6 per cent) of the adolescents' total waking time was spent involved in sports. When this figure of 6 per cent was broken down, it revealed that a significant majority of adolescents (70 per cent) were actually involved in informal sports. There were broadly similar findings documented by De Knop et al (1996) in their exploration and comparison of twenty countries across the globe and documented in *Worldwide Trends in Youth Sport*. Perhaps the minimal time expenditure by adolescents in sport, as documented in these studies, accounts for the limited amount of empirical research on the sporting activities of this age group.

Physical activities/sport clearly do not dominate the life experiences of many adolescents. However, for those who are active, partaking in physical activities/sport appears to be offering some of the most positive experiences during adolescence. For example, for many adolescents, taking part in sporting activities was one of their favourite aspects of school. A significant minority engaged in a variety of sporting activities both inside and outside the school environment and claimed to enjoy this participation for a variety of physical and social reasons.

If adolescents are generally positive about their sporting activities, why then does this not translate into higher levels of participation? There would appear to be a number of key reasons for this anomaly. Lifestyle and time issues would appear to determine participation levels. The time available for physical activity is increasingly being eroded by the time needed to partake in a variety of other leisure and lifestyle patterns. In particular, home-based leisure activities are increasingly impacting on the amount of time available for physical activity (De Knop et al, 1996). In this instance, the increasing availability of satellite and digital television and access to computer games and the Internet has meant that the time available for sporting activities has been displaced by these sedentary pursuits. The challenges facing youth sport and the changing nature of adolescence appear to be increasingly acknowledged by many sports administrators. O'Reilly (2000)[1] stated that:

> In the past, kids were naturally fit but modern day kids live in a TV/video/Playstation world and are now naturally unfit. They live in an isolation activity world and sports administrators and coaches must be aware of that.

Trevor Brooking, Chief Executive of Sport England,[2] also acknowledges the challenges faced by sporting organisations (in this instance, Association Football):

> In recent years, it has been very noticeable that, while the children turn up in much more expensive kit than ever before, they can hardly kick a ball . . . these kids have nobody to teach them. The maths teacher who used to take the football team after school or at weekends doesn't do it anymore. But there is no use looking back and asking why. We have to rethink and put in place completely new structures.

Another key factor that is impinging on participation rates in traditional sports is the increasing participation in casual leisure and sporting activities by adolescents. Hendry (1978, 1989, and 1993) has written extensively on the changing focuses of interest and types of leisure pursuit patterns amongst adolescents. Hendry argues that the focus of teenagers generally shifts from adult-organised clubs and activities (c. thirteen years old), through

---

[1] Unpublished paper given by Noel Reilly, Assistant Youth Team Manager and Regional Development Officer with the Football Association of Ireland at a national coaching seminar organised by the FAI, January 2000.

[2] Quoted in *The Sunday Times*, September 1999.

casual leisure pursuits (c. fifteen years old) to commercially organised leisure (c. seventeen years old). This research has
shown a similar flow pattern in the lifestyle interests of adolescents and this may be the main contributing factor to increasing
dropout from traditional organised sport as the adolescent gets
older. It would appear that the traditional diet of organised team
and individual sports appeals primarily to the younger adolescent and will not maintain the interest of many older adolescents.

Fitzclarence and Tinning (1992) give an interesting review of
some of their qualitative research with adolescents and PE
teachers in Australia. They outline an example that appears to
summarise a number of the key issues. In this case, three girls
attended PE classes twice a week but their teacher felt they did
not show much enthusiasm for physical education. In fact, one of
them said she hated PE. What was amazing in this case was that
the same three girls came to private classes in the local gym
which were run by the same teacher and took part in aerobics,
worked out in the gym doing weight training or had a swim. In
the view of these researchers, there is an apparent disjunction
between school physical education and sport and the lives of
adolescent youth. Many adolescents appear bored with school
physical education and sport provision, yet they are serious
about the place of physical activity in their out-of-school lives.

Adolescents make choices regarding their leisure and sporting activities from a range of lifestyle patterns that are compati-
ble with their present contexts or ways of life and their perception of themselves. The stability and any changes in their leisure
behaviour may be related to a way of life or context. When contexts change or transition occurs, a multitude of changes, both
within the individual and within the social environment, will occur (Silbereisen et al., 1992). Resources, opportunities and role
expectations all change within a life transition. Transitional periods, especially adolescence, are important in terms of the stability and change in sporting, leisure and lifestyle patterns.

Adolescence is a "critical life phase" (Brodie, 1992). It has
been well established in leisure research that roughly one-half of
adults' current leisure activities are begun in childhood and
early adolescence (Lounsbury and Hoopes, 1988; Scott and Willits, 1989; Iso-Ahola, 1994; Jackson and Dunn, 1988). Therefore,

the study of the sporting, leisure and lifestyle patterns of adolescents is important from both the individual and societal standpoint. Such research helps shed light on active versus passive leisure lifestyles and their impact on the person and society. The ways in which young people shape their lifestyle is currently more difficult to analyse and predict because political, social and moral values have become more diffuse as Ireland has become a more pluralist society. Having reflected on the above, it would appear that there are a number of emerging themes which encapsulate the key areas of the sporting, leisure and lifestyle patterns of adolescents. These themes are now discussed for what they can illuminate in relation to the sporting, leisure and lifestyle patterns of school-going Waterford adolescents.

EMERGENT THEMES

The lifestyle analysis conducted in this research points not only to clear social class and gender differences but also to important lifestyle variations within and across social class boundaries as young people make their decisions about sport and physical activity. Adolescent lifestyles appear to be clearly differentiated across a range of factors including leisure and sporting interests. Hendry et al. (1993) summarise this complex relation when they claim that

> there can be a mixture of self perceptions, motivations, meanings and saliences that individual adolescents place upon various social and leisure activities which interact with social influences such as living conditions, parenting styles and family units, school peer groups and facets of wider cultural effects such as the mass media (p. 186).

Whilst elaborating on general trends is fraught with problems in the context of each individual adolescent's decision in relation to sport and physical activity, nevertheless it would appear from this research that there are a number of definite trends which should be borne in mind by people and bodies interested in the promotion and provision of physical activity and youth sport.

Trend 1 — Increasing Difficulty in Providing for the Needs of Youth Sport

There are several problems identified in the provision of physical activity/sport issues which arose in the course of this research but a general trend would appear to be that schools and sporting organisations are finding it increasingly difficult to provide for the sporting and physical activity needs of adolescents. Some of the key issues would be a lack of time amongst providers, increasing bureaucracy, a decline in the numbers of volunteers, increasing professionalisation of sport, crisis in school physical education and a perception that teenagers are more demanding.

Lack of Time

Increased economic pressure, time demands and two trends in family systems in Ireland — namely the increasing levels of maternal employment and greater paternal involvement in child-rearing — appear to be making it increasingly difficult for the traditional provider of sport (males) to commit as much time as they previously would have to youth sport. Many sporting organisations are thus finding it difficult to provide coaches or organisers for their youth sports. For example, in 1999 three youth soccer teams had to pull out of leagues in Waterford because they had no one to take charge of them.

Increasing Bureaucracy

Many of the initiatives by the government and sporting bodies in recent years in relation to youth sport have been welcomed. These initiatives have included new regulations in relation to child protection that were established to prevent further cases of the high-profile childhood sexual abuse in sport which came to the fore in the 1990s. The net effect of these and other initiatives have meant that coaches and youth leaders are now operating under a more bureaucratic regime. Some of the demands that are proving difficult include the compulsory training or coaching programmes that coaches have to undertake. Coaches are often required to have a second parent or volunteer (often of a different sex) present at their training sessions. All volunteers have to be vetted by the police and systems for reporting problems have to be followed. There is also increased bureaucracy in relation to insurance which includes the increasing paperwork necessary to comply with insurance requirements or reporting accidents. Added to the above, the coach or volunteer often has to collect money from adolescents for a variety of costs including insurance, facilities, equipment, coaching, transport and affiliation to national bodies. They may also have to apply for grants from the relevant local authority and be involved in fundraising. All of these requirements are a big turn-off for many coaches and sports administrators who, in many instances, claim to spend as much time on paperwork as on coaching.

The Increasing Professionalisation of Sport and Teenagers becoming more Demanding

Many adolescents are being exposed to professional sports providers from an early age. Examples would include PE personnel or qualified coaches and what they see on the media. What this has meant is that it is increasingly difficult for the casual volunteer to compete for and maintain the interests of adolescents. One long-time youth leader summed up his perspective:

> When I started in youth work 25 years ago, all you had to do was call a meeting and then come along and throw in a ball when the youth club started. The kids nowadays are used to better and would be gone in a couple of weeks if you didn't prepare and structure activities for them.

A proliferation of courses introduced in Ireland during the 1990s produced graduates in various areas of sports and recreation. In the 1980s, only two third-level colleges had courses in the sport and physical education areas. Since then, six new courses have come on stream in the institute of technology sector, four in the university sector and over thirty courses in the post-Leaving Certificate course area with several more in the pipeline. The National Coaching and Training Centre has standardised and professionalised coaching standards in conjunction with the national governing bodies. This professionalisation of the sport and leisure industry has meant that in many instances volunteers are working with professionals for the first time. The attendant problems of professional versus non-professional delivery of services and the likelihood of the professional being paid while the volunteer is not are difficult dilemmas that many sporting organisations are currently facing.

There also appears to be an increasing trend towards individualisation amongst adolescents (Beckers, 1989; Roberts and Kamphorst, 1989). Adolescents' behaviour and preferences are now less determined by traditional links with their family, their local area and local sports. Their leisure behaviour is now more influenced by personal choice, and sports such as the Gaelic games, with their ethos of loyalty to local club and parish, may find that these factors may not motivate adolescents to remain loyal as would have been the traditional expectation. Other issues noted by youth leaders was a perceived increase in social problems and discipline issues and a number commented on the perceived decreasing attention span of many adolescents which was often attributed to the influence of television.

Issues in School Physical Education

Some of the issues facing school physical education include lack of time, curriculum overload, role conflict between teaching and coaching, lack of facilities, over-stretched teachers, low subject status, lack of financial support and a shortage of staff to provide the types of programmes that would help educate a higher percentage of adolescents to become and remain physically active. Many of these factors appear to be affecting the morale of the physical educators. Some PE teachers would like to provide a different type of PE programme but are constricted by the above reasons. PE as a subject is likely to be introduced as an examinable subject in Irish schools in the coming years but whether this initiative will solve the problems within PE in the future is debatable. This issue should be discussed in depth by all the stake holders involved in the provision of PE in second-level schools including representatives from teachers, parents, school management, students, Department of Education and Science and the PE Association of Ireland.

A Decline in the Number of Volunteers

This issue is closely related to a number of the above points. Schools and sporting organisations are finding it increasingly difficult to find volunteers who have to date been an intrinsic part of youth sport. Many people involved in youth sport talk about aspects such as the nature of their service now being a babysitting service, with parents dumping their children and running. The lack of volunteers has meant increased transport costs in having to hire buses, having to pull teams out of competitions, games called off due to a lack of officials and sometimes no one to coach certain teams. The increasing secularisation of Irish education has also meant that the commitment traditionally given to some sports by members of religious orders is rapidly dying. Examples would include the role of Christian Brothers in promoting Gaelic games, the role of the Jesuit order and the Holy Ghost priests and brothers in promoting rugby.

Trend 2 — Gender Issues

On the positive side, there would appear to be a definite trend towards democratisation of provision for both boys and girls, but significant inequalities do still exist. The socialisation process into sport clearly still encourages more boys than girls into sport. However, there would appear to be a growing awareness of gender issues in sports provision. A good example of this would be the review of the Primary School Curriculum in 1998/99, where there is now an emphasis on gender equity. In the view of a primary school inspector who was involved in the review process, this was particularly true in relation to PE as opposed to other subject areas. He claimed that

> there had been particularly, in the seventies and eighties, a tacit acceptance that there were a lot of PE activities which were considered to be male only with the exception of sports like camogie and hockey. The emphasis is now on all schools to provide equity in PE provision for both genders. This is particularly important as there are now far more mixed sex than single sex schools in Ireland.

Similarly, at second level, some girls now appear to have opportunities to play traditional male sports like soccer and to have access to other activities such as outdoor pursuits.

The forms of discrimination currently being practised appear more subtle and less conspicuous. This research supports the finding of Lynch, who in her review of facilities and extra-curricular provision in Irish schools, found that

> the bias in girls' schools towards the arts and other home related activities shows how the extra curricular life of the school reinforces gender stereotypes. Girls are more likely to have facilities for crafts or general purpose halls (1989, p. 119).

Sex stereotyping still exists and young girls' lack of exposure to a variety of sports (e.g. rugby) may result in a self-selection away from what may be considered as inappropriate activities. In general, the provision for girls in certain sports like basketball, hockey and swimming appears reasonable, but the provision of traditional male sports in particular appears to lag far behind the perceived demand.

Trend 3 — Increased Competition from Alternative Leisure Pursuits

The time available for adolescents to partake in sport or physical activity would appear to be eroded and displaced by time spent on the ICT. It would appear that this trend is likely to be exacerbated in the coming years. For example, mobile phones achieved the greatest sales growth of any technology consumer item in the world in 1999.[3] Now almost 100 per cent of teenagers have mobile phones. In 1996, 5 per cent of Irish adults had access to the Internet and three years later this figure had reached 33 per cent[4] and has risen consistently since. The advent of attractions such as digital television, DVD and future technological developments is likely to mean that more and more time is spent on the ICT which will impact on the time

---

[3] 100,000 mobile phones were sold in Ireland over the Christmas period at the end of 1999.

[4] Business Section, *Sunday Times*, January 2000.

adolescents have for sporting and other activities. The competition for adolescents' time in the coming years is likely to be even more intense.

Trend 4 — Democratisation of Access to Sporting Opportunities

There would appear to be a trend towards democratisation across the socio-economic class groupings in relation to their sporting activities. However, there are still many differences among the various groups in society and most of these differences favour the higher socio-economic classes. The findings from this study replicate the findings of Lynch, who found that the social class composition of the school has a considerable bearing on the provision of extracurricular facilities. Schools with the largest cohort of pupils from higher-income groups overall have the best facilities. The hidden curriculum is particularly significant according to Lynch (1989). She particularly notes the effects of extracurricular provision, which is at the school's discretion and lies outside the remit of state control. According to Lynch, "the extracurricular life of schools reproduces class and gender traditions in a variety of cultural spheres" (1989, p. 116). The link between gender and class is significant. While working-class boys were almost as active as middle-class boys, the biggest difference in participation levels was between working-class girls, who had low levels of participation, and middle-class girls, who were almost on a par with middle-class boys. A similar story existed outside of the school setting. Students from the higher socio-economic groups had greater access to a wider variety of sport and physical activities in their neighbourhood, more access to transport, increased money for activities and knowledge of a greater variety of activities than their working-class counterparts. It is not surprising, therefore, that in general adolescents from the higher socio-economic groups are advantaged in their access to and use of sporting facilities and equipment.

At an aggregate level, factors such as age, sex, education and social class groupings filter out the potentially active from the probably passive. Thus, the general social structure largely determines, at an aggregate level, the number of adolescents who will be physically active. Since broad social policy may slowly change these structures in a population, this may over time affect the numbers participating in sport. Factors such as age, sex, education and social class groupings do not determine the decision of the individual. But they have their effect, in probability terms, upon groups of individuals with particular social attributes. These individual decisions are made by a process outlined in Figure 10.1 below. Aggregated at the group level, these innumerable personal decisions are reflected in the influence of social attributes on participation levels.

Trend 5 — The Decision to Participate: The Social Filters

There are a whole series of social filters that will limit the number of adolescents who will participate in sport. For example, an eighteen-year working-class girl with few sporting skills is likely to be inactive. Similarly, a twelve-year-old middle-class boy who is good at sports is likely to be an active sports participant. The filters are outlined in the following figure.

Figure 10.1: Adolescents and Sports Participation — the Social Filters

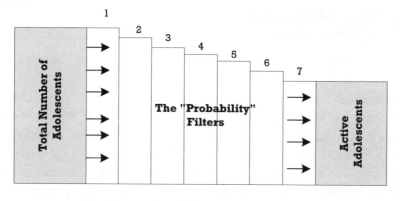

(Not in any rank order)

1. Age   5. Competence
2. Sex   6. Socialisation process
3. Education level   7. Urban/Rural
4. Social class grouping

Source: Adapted from a concept in a paper by Greg Knipe, University of Limerick, 1991.

SPORTS PARTICIPATION MODEL — CORE GROUPS WITH VARYING INTEREST LEVELS IN PHYSICAL ACTIVITY AND SPORT

Having examined the factors which affect participation levels, a model of sports participation by adolescents is now outlined. The following model presents a generalised description of adolescent sport and activity levels by adolescents. Of course, there are many local variations and, for example, the activity levels can differ greatly for a myriad of reasons. However, the following description appears to apply to the general cohort of adolescents.

Figure 10.2: Likelihood of Participation

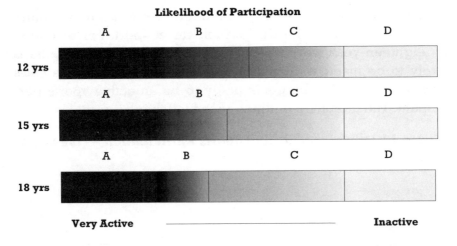

Adolescents' interest in participating in sport and physical activity can be divided into four groups, each of which would roughly represent one quarter of the adolescent population. Group A could be classified as the core group of active adolescents who in many cases have high activity levels either in one sport or across a variety of sports. Members of this group would tend to stay active right across their adolescent years and probably into adulthood. A member of Group B could be described as being likely to be active. This group would be generally comprised of those adolescents who enjoy sport and would actively participate in PE, sporting clubs and casual sports. They would be particularly active in early adolescence but would be less active as they get older and members of this group would be more likely to dabble in a variety of sports than to be loyal to one particular sport. Some of this group would be expected to drop away from sport as they move through adolescence and into adulthood.

Group C could be described as the drop-out group. Members of this group would probably be active in their early adolescent years, particularly as they enter the second-level school system. For a variety of reasons, group members become inactive as they progress through adolescence with the highest drop-out rates occurring around the time of their Junior Certificate examination. By the time they are leaving second-level education, they are likely to be inactive. Group D members could be described as the core inactive group. These students are likely to be inactive from before or around early adolescence. They would probably only take part in compulsory physical activities such as physical education classes. Members of this group are not active and will drop out of all physical activities as soon as they have that choice. This group, comprising 25 per cent of the adolescent population, remains fairly constant in size through adolescence.

This model shows clearly that at age twelve, 75 per cent are active while by age eighteen less than 50 per cent are active. Members of Group A at twelve are going to be active participants no matter what level of provision is provided to them by schools or clubs — again, the size of this group will remain fairly constant through adolescence. However, Group C members at twelve come into secondary active and are inactive when they leave. Therefore considerable numbers of adolescents are dropping out from sport during their adolescent years. The finding from this research supports contemporary research findings with young people attending second-level schooling. These findings suggest that young people are becoming less active as they progress through their school years (Armstrong and McManus, 1994b). The findings also support research results from Sutherland (1992) who found that post-primary aged students in their mid-teens were dropping out of sport with girls much more likely to drop out than boys.

A number of comments can be made in relation to the provision of sport and physical activity to members of the above groups. The first is that in the area of physical activity promotion and provision, the education system and sporting organisations specifically target the available resources at a percentage of adolescents, namely members of Groups A and B and these make up only half of the adolescent population. On the other hand, the specific needs of an unacceptably high level of adolescents are not being met. In order to provide for their needs, a judicious shift is needed away from what currently happens. The second comment is that the problem often is on the supply side rather than with the individual student. This research demonstrates that the majority of the inactive group are not in fact averse to the concept of physical activity with about three-quarters of early adolescents being active in sport and physical activity. However, the total physical activity experience of these students in the school setting does not promote positive attitudes to physical activity. The traditional team games appear to be widely available in both primary and second-level schools. However, for the older adolescent, or the adolescent who is not interested in games, the choice is often bleak. There needs to be increased availability of opportunities for casual leisure activities. Schools, sports organisations and parents appear keen to provide organised and supervised activities while many adolescents want casual activities. Currently, never the twain shall meet. To seriously address the issue of physical activity patterns, opportunities for casual sports participation need to be available for adolescents. Adolescents also need to be involved in the drawing-up and planning of programmes. Similarly, as adolescents are more individualistic in their tastes, there needs to be greater elements of choice in programme provision. Alternative programmes need to be designed and delivered to meet the needs of the currently inactive students.

The school setting and sporting clubs are supportive of those who are good at sport, i.e. the motor elite and the achievement-oriented students. The total physical activity experience in the school setting and/or sports clubs, for many of these students, is very positive. The physical education class, which has been shown to favour team games and competitive activities, amply meets their needs. The extracurricular provision again favours this cohort who are good at sport and enjoy winning. If they play on school teams, many resources are provided for them in the form of coaching, transport and financial support. Furthermore, they enjoy all the rewards of success, such as having their photographs hung on the school walls and being mentioned in reports in local newspapers. Thus, it is not surprising to find that some students play on as many as three school teams and these same students often play with a similar number of teams with outside sporting clubs.

In parallel with this elite cohort, there are other groups for which the same physical activity experience is counterproductive. The school ethos, the PE classes and extracurricular provision and sporting clubs appear to constrain their participation. Their needs are very different yet very few resources are directed at these students. Perhaps this is because their needs appear to lie within the area of casual leisure and sports providers find difficulty in catering for these needs. It is not surprising therefore to find that many of them either do not take part or withdraw from physical activity altogether. Inclusion rather than exclusion must be the goal, particularly in the school setting.

SUMMARY

This chapter has presented an overview of the findings in relation to the sporting, leisure and lifestyle patterns of adolescents. Having presented the key findings, a series of emerging trends in physical activity and youth sport participation by these same adolescents was outlined. It appears clear from this research that there is a wide divergence between the public perception of the level of physical activity engaged in by adolescents and the actual reality. A feature of postmodern adolescent lifestyle patterns is that their lifestyle often includes television, the Internet, mobile phones, fashion, rock music, drinking and dance, and that for many adolescents sport/physical activity is not part of their lifestyle. These are the cultural forms that are the expressive channels of this generation. This book has attempted to map the life world of adolescents.

Anyone interested in promoting physical activity/sport ignores this life world at their peril. If we can understand adolescents' life world, it may be easier to design and adapt sport/physical activity provision to ensure that this becomes part of the leisure and lifestyle patterns of significantly more of them. The final chapter will now examine some of the policy issues that impact on the sporting and physical activity patterns of adolescents.

Chapter 11

POLICY ISSUES IN RELATION TO THE PROVISION OF SPORT FOR YOUNG PEOPLE

The findings from the research give an indication of the extent of commitment to sport by young people. They also provide baseline data against which the broad impact of existing programmes and informing policies can be assessed. The purpose of this chapter is to briefly consider policy issues that may affect the sporting levels of adolescents. Providing positive sporting experiences for the many in this new millennium poses several challenges for those involved in developing policies and also for those charged with their implementation. The 1990s in Ireland were a time of rapid change. As Brennan (2000) recounts:

> Sociologists will look back at the 1990s in Ireland and say it was a very large laboratory experiment in fast-track social change. Ireland has undergone economic, social and cultural changes in five to ten years that other societies underwent in twenty-five or thirty years. No change like that happens without someone or something suffering.[1]

This era of rapid change in society in general has also impacted on sport. However, what is new in the Irish context is that, at this time and for the first time, a number of the key policy providers have implemented strategies to specifically develop sport.

These developments, which will impact on Irish sport in the coming years, include:

---

[1] From an article in the *Irish Independent*, January 2000.

- The Irish Sports Council, which was established as a statutory body in June 1999;

- The physical education programme in primary schools was reviewed in 1999 and piloted in schools in 2002/3;

- PE in second-level schools may become an exam subject by the middle to end of this decade.

There are therefore several areas of public policy that are in their infancy and it is thus too soon to evaluate their success but this chapter will make some general comments in relation to sports policy in Ireland as it impacts on adolescents and evaluate the foundations on which some of the above policies are built.

As already discussed, the decision to participate in sports and physical activity is determined by larger processes of social relations encompassing gender, ethnicity and social class groupings. Sports are themselves part of social and cultural formations and cannot ultimately be separated from the economic and political practices that often constrain or encourage people's choices and activities. Socialisation through sport cannot be approached in terms of unreflective responses to certain events, relationships and external forces. As Coakley states:

> sports participation is a socially constructed process mediated by power relations and the consciousness and collective reflection of participants (1996, p. 361).

Therefore, whilst it is useful to target certain key groups such as working-class girls, it is also important to take a holistic view in promoting increased sporting and physical activity patterns amongst adolescents. This means that in many instances a whole range of constraints may have to be tackled to help promote higher physical activity patterns amongst certain groups of adolescents.

Simplistic solutions like the provision of extra facilities may not necessarily increase participation rates in sport by teenagers. In many instances, such facilities would not be used by non-active adolescents. The value placed on physical activity by the adolescent will normally dictate if they adopt an active lifestyle pattern. However, even when the adolescent places a high value on being physically active, other factors may mean that they are not physically active. For example, an adolescent may weigh up the cost and benefits of their present situation to determine whether to remain involved in or withdraw from sport/physical activity. Thus, an older adolescent may not partake in any activity because they want to spend more time studying to get the college place of their choice or they may want to work part-time to be financially independent. As the adolescent has many choices, the implementation of the following policies may help to increase the likelihood of more adolescents becoming or remaining physically active across the adolescent years.

GENDER ISSUES

Physical and gender differences need to be taken into account when designing sports programmes. A common approach to providing sports programmes for both boys and girls may be ineffective in the light of their different activity interests, motives, values, perceptions and abilities. Girls tend to be socialised into indoor activities and as many of their interests lie in this area, greater efforts to increase the activity levels of girls should include activities which can be based in and from the home and these should be further emphasised. These would include home exercises, walking and jogging. Experimentation also needs to take place with the provision of the PE programme to establish whether mixed, segregated or sometimes mixed classes are the most effective means of encouraging more girls to be physically active. One PE teacher, who had participation rates of between 80 and 90 per cent by senior-cycle girls in an all-girls' school (located in a working-class area), was of the view that all senior-cycle programming should be based on recreational and individual sports. He attributed the success of the programme to the nature of the activities which were on offer, to the time allocated to the PE programme and to the variety and choice of activities available. These activities included circuit training, walking, weights, squash, self-defence, swimming and social trips away to outdoor pursuits centres. The right type of programmes could, in his view, support much higher participation rates in sport by girls than is currently the case in many schools.

In a mixed-class situation, it may be better to offer gender-neutral activities like swimming initially and to offer strongly stereotyped activities like rugby in single-sex groupings. Early exposure to strongly stereotyped sports before self-consciousness becomes an issue (i.e. in the primary school years) may help to eliminate the sexual stereotyping of some sports. But, above all, schools need to promote the achievements of girls on an equal footing with boys. Currently, it would appear that for many girls, school work takes priority over sports. Eccles and Harold (1991) claimed that girls saw themselves as being less able in sport than boys and indicated that doing well in school subjects was more important than doing well in sports. Watson (1996) showed that girls spent longer on homework than boys and there has been a clear trend in recent years in Ireland for girls to outperform boys in state examinations. Many girls are being socialised into non-sporting roles by a variety of latent forces in the current school setting. Lynch (1989) documents some of the influences of the hidden curriculum to include:

- The general lack of certain sporting facilities in girls' schools;

- The types of extracurricular activities provided for girls;

- The bias in girls' schools towards the arts and other home-related activities;

- The increased availability of facilities for crafts in girls' schools (pp. 112–115).

These issues need to be addressed if sport is to be accepted fully in schools as being a core part of the gender role socialisation process for girls.

PROGRAMME ISSUES

Enjoyment needs to become the principal outcome of sports and PE programmes with young people. Sports provision appears to have become more bureaucratic, more structured, more professional, more restrictive, more institutionalised and more interested in the better athletes. As the above factors are primary contributors to sport withdrawal by young people, a fundamental shift is needed to make sport more enjoyable with fun, mini and casual games coming more to the forefront. Likewise, there needs to be a greater emphasis on physical activities which are potentially lifelong activities. Even in primary schools in Ireland, there is evidence that the games culture is supported, and this research has shown that the games culture is clearly dominant in second-level schools. What happens in the primary school setting will often influence subsequent events in second-level schools and as a result some general comments will now be made in relation to primary school physical education and sport.

Currently in Irish primary education, the delivery of the PE programme is the responsibility of each individual teacher. The reality is that, in many instances, what is actually purported to be the physical education programme is carried out by coaches from the various national governing bodies of sport. In many instances, there are full-time hurling and football coaches who visit schools to teach hurling and football. Coaches are also involved in soccer, swimming and rugby programmes. Similarly, a study (Crowley, 2000) of 40 primary school teachers in three primary schools in Waterford City found that over 50 per cent did not feel confident teaching physical education. Interestingly, 10 per cent claimed that they had received no training in the teaching of physical education during their own training. Over half the teachers also felt that there was a need for a PE specialist in the primary school setting. From the point of view of policy, it would appear that there is a clear need to analyse both the type of sports provision given in primary schools and also the training provided for those who deliver the PE programmes in primary education. It could be argued, for example, that a hurling coach is ultimately only interested in attracting as many hurlers as possible into the game of hurling and, as a result, is unlikely to be interested in the physical development of each child. There is also the question of the quality of an experience which can be offered by a Level One[2] coach as compared to a trained PE teacher. Currently, an association between sport and team games is being given to children from an early age. This is giving students a blinkered view of the nature of sport and may be giving negative experiences of sport to a significant minority. In reality, many of those students who are not interested in team games may be turned away from any future type of sports participation.

The other policy issue that warrants discussion at a national level is whether or not PE teachers would be more usefully employed in primary schools rather than (or as well as) second-level schools as is the case at present. The physical competencies that a child brings from primary to second-level school are likely to determine whether or not that child is physically active. The recent innovations in physical education and sports provision in both Australia and New Zealand appear to have been particularly successful in increasing the participation rates in sport by their youths. The programmes on offer in these countries differ considerably from what appears to be currently on offer in Irish schools. Whilst there are no figures available for the Irish Republic, Ogle (1997) cites how only 1 per cent of children in Northern Ireland had any experience of mini-sport. This compares with modified games or mini-sports that have an almost universal acceptance in Australia and New Zealand, with over 90 per cent of schools delivering modified games. Thus, it is the way in which sport is introduced and developed that may increase lifelong participation rates. Currently, the programmes in Ireland appear to be concentrating on the traditional team games even in primary school and a fundamental rethink may be necessary as to how sport is introduced in Irish schools.

Whilst it is too early to offer an evaluation of the role of the Irish Sports Council, which became a statutory body in the summer of 1999, their early focus has clearly been on the development of elite sports people. This is one of the four areas that

---

[2] The National Coaching and Training Centre in Limerick certifies people with varying levels of coaching awards. The Level One award is the lowest and involves a short training period but it is accepted as appropriate in many school settings.

are targeted in the Government Act that made them a statutory body. However, the development of recreational sports has also been highlighted as a core strategy in the Act. A paper given by Paul McDermott of the Irish Sports Council in February 2000, in Waterford,[3] outlined that the Sports Council did not have the necessary resources to tackle the four areas mentioned in the Act. They had, to date, concentrated their resources on two areas: namely, elite sport and a strategy to combat performance-enhancing drug-taking in sport that again focuses primarily on elite athletes. Whilst the Sports Council intends to develop policies to promote recreational sport, their policies to date have been clearly functionalist in nature. The Government wants to have Irish athletes competing on a world stage and apparently scarce resources are being targeted at a select few. There is a strong argument that elite athletes are already advantaged and that the real need for sports provision lies not with elite athletes but with the less active and the disadvantaged.

This theme of promoting the elite athlete also appears to dominate the provision for youth sport in schools. Schools often appear to be associated with one sport and this one sport for the few is targeted at the expense of the many who do not make the school teams. It is felt to be important for schools to have winning teams. This view appears to be supported by school management and teaching staff, by parents, by the local press and wider society and would appear to be given greater priority than a policy to have participation by the mass pupil population. The role of school teams and the practice of selecting teams deserves special attention. For those who wish to play in organised sport, there should be leagues to cater for their level of ability. For most schools, even amongst those who would aspire to have more students involved on their teams, there are resource issues, particularly in relation to getting suitable volunteers to give their time to school teams. This is significant as coaches are interested in winning and few want to be involved with the non-elite athletes. A move to targeting more resources

[3] Paper presented at the Recreation Management Graduate Conference, Waterford Institute of Technology, February 2000.

at intra-school sports would be one way of addressing the needs of more students.

There are a number of sports initiatives currently in operation that may be worth developing. For example, one sport that has embraced the democratising concept is golf; the handicap system has meant that all golfers can compete at their own level and win competitions against technically superior golfers. This may be the core reason why golf is increasingly becoming more popular as a lifelong activity. Golfers can compete at all levels from just for fun and social reasons to the highest competitive level, depending on the individual golfer's interest and ability. It is a highly successful concept that can be adapted by other sports. Orienteering is another sport that embraces this concept. The Dublin Primary schools GAA also have an innovative system. They invite players from several schools to open competitions and teams are drawn out of a hat and then play each other, wearing an allocated county team's colours. All students get to play and students from stronger and weaker schools are competing on a level playing field. These competitions are extremely popular with the students who are involved. Other simple initiatives include having to play each member of a team for a specified number of minutes in each game and to have mixed teams.

The strategies used in Australia and New Zealand in teaching sport through modified games and mini-sport need to be examined and applied, if deemed suitable, in an Irish context. The Irish Rugby Union already use this concept in their Leprechaun rugby but the need to apply this type of sports teaching right across the whole school years needs to be examined. To date, the concept of mini-sport appears to have been highly successful in increasing participation rates in sport in New Zealand and Australia (Collins and Trenberth, 1994). This shift in emphasis on how sport is introduced also needs to happen if efforts to achieve increased participation levels by the adolescents are to be successful.

SOCIAL CLASS GROUPING ISSUES

Far from being innate, adolescents learn lifestyle and sporting preferences and the process of learning is contoured along class lines. Access to valued sporting goods and services are restricted and the power chances of particular classes of individuals are contoured by what Bourdieu (1986) refers to as the volume of *capital* that they possess. This capital is not just economic, but is also cultural (e.g. education, knowledge of high culture and arts and symbolic). Bourdieu also claims that the choice of learning a sport or leisure activity is not a question of free choice and individual taste. The choice is socially structured, reflecting the possession and deployment of varying degrees and combinations of economic, cultural and symbolic capital. Indeed, evidence from this research and from across the world (Ogle, 1994) shows a clear association between higher socio-economic status and participation in sport. As a result, sporting participation may reflect, and even exaggerate, disparities amongst social class groupings.

Both within the school environment and because of where they live, the higher social class groupings will have increased access to sporting facilities, to a wider range of activities, to better facilities, to more coaching and more money to spend on sporting activities. In the Republic of South Africa, sport has been adopted as a means of promoting a new democratic ethos, as a unifier and healer of wounds and redeemer of marginalised youth (Department of Sport and Recreation, RSA, 1995). While these grandiose ideals are noble, the reality of democratising sport is far more difficult. Some of the constraints to working-class adolescents' participation in sport can be readily tackled. The varying levels of sports facilities in differing types of schools, as documented by Lynch, can be tackled to some extent by the Department of Education and Science if they provide a certain basic level of facilities to all schools. Middle-class schools would still have greater economic resources through their ability to fundraise but the gap in facility provision would be reduced between the different school types if the Department of Education and Science introduced this measure.

The Irish Sports Council has acknowledged that there are lower participation rates in sport by those individuals from the lower social class groupings. As a result, one of the strategic goals set for sport in the Department of Tourism, Sport and Recreation's statement of strategy 1998–2001 is

> to formulate and oversee the implementation of policies for the promotion and development of sport, and to encourage increased participation in sport and recreation, particularly by disadvantaged communities (2000, p. 2).

However, the means of achieving this goal, particularly in relation to improving the participation rates by disadvantaged communities, appears to be based solely on increased levels of monetary grants to those groups who are considered to be disadvantaged. The Irish Sports Council's approach appears to be grounded in a deprivation hypothesis theoretical framework. They see a close link between the lack of physical resources, particularly sports facilities, and subsequent participation levels in sport. The evidence from this research is that this view is fundamentally flawed and, in fact, this represents only one of a number of issues which need to be resolved if the participation rates in sport by those from the lower social class grouping are to be increased. A major function of any sports programme design is to ensure that the participation levels of the varying social class groupings are maximised and this needs much greater attention. It does appear that different types of programmes have differing levels of success in maintaining or increasing participation levels by those from the lower social class groupings.

The results from this research suggest an anomaly which appears difficult to reconcile. On the one hand, it could be suggested that education is the answer to many of the issues involved in the lower participation rates in sports by adolescents from lower social class groupings. Many of the constraints to sports participation can be tackled, in theory, by a good education programme. Through the educational process, for example, adolescents from lower social class groupings could be exposed to a variety of sports, thus broadening their mental maps. Similarly, through school sports and other school-related activities, they could be afforded opportunities to travel and to broaden their minds. Thirdly, through education, it would be expected that their self-esteem would be increased and that they would be more confident in themselves. School could also provide opportunities for adolescents to learn physical skills and to increase their competencies in a variety of sporting activities.

The anomaly, however, is that the institution of the school appears to be, on the one hand, fulfilling the sporting needs of the higher social class and, on the other, alienating many adolescents from the lower social class groupings. Schools support middle-class values. The Conference of Religious in Ireland believes that "the values of Irish schools, particularly at second level, are those of individualism, competitiveness and consumerism which are manifested by the points race and the 'mé féin' free market" (Pollak, 1998, p. 5). In the Irish scenario, it would appear that, in the cases of many non-active adolescents from the lower social class groupings, their social needs must be addressed before they are likely to be active in sports. Currently, youth centres are carrying out much good work in this area, with many of the successful programmes offering a variety of casual sports, generally, in a social context. Schools need to learn from the work carried out by some youth centres and to change their ethos to accommodate the sporting needs of adolescents from the lower social class groupings. The increased use of mini-games and an emphasis on the social aspects of the sporting experiences provided would be likely to make sports participation in school more attractive to students from the lower social class groupings.

EPILOGUE

Many of the issues discussed in this research can be summed up in this quote from Michener's classic treatise from 1976, *Sports in America*:

> We just don't teach boys and girls the right sports in school, the ones they will enjoy during their adult lives . . . it is ironic, and a consequence of our adult attitudes that the two sports (baseball and football) on which we have spent the most effort and money on young boys are the ones they will not be able to use in adult life (1976, p. 140).

Whilst the sports mentioned are obviously American, close parallels may be drawn with the main team sports that are prevalent in Ireland. It would appear that, in the Irish context at the start of a new millennium, the above sentiments, as expressed by Michener, are as relevant today as they were in the United States in the mid-1970s. This book has discussed the sporting, leisure and lifestyle patterns of school-going adolescents. The nature of Irish society is changing rapidly. The greatest challenge facing those drafting and implementing sports policy is how to adapt the concept of sport to suit the needs of the vast majority of adolescents rather than the selected few, as is currently the case. To do this, a strategic move from an emphasis on provision to the promotion of participation levels by the general body of adolescents has to occur. The uptake of sport is linked to these two separate but closely linked issues. From the research undertaken, a number of strong arguments have emerged in relation to both these areas and these will now be briefly outlined.

The provision of sporting opportunities is often determined at a local level. These will often depend on localised decisions such as, for example, whether an individual school decides to fundraise for a sports hall or a computer laboratory. The influence of local public representatives, local lobby groups, the local media, the ability of the local community to fundraise and the success of particular sports in a local area will all affect local decisions. Some interesting examples in the Waterford context include the decision of the local authority to build and run a golf course but not to provide a swimming pool for their residents. Similarly, the local authority received money from central government to build an athletics track. However, due to local lobbying, this has now become the home venue for the local city soccer team and the athletics track is seldom used. In most cases, therefore, the key determinants of particular provision levels for sport are decided by localised factors.

The issue of participation levels, as an area of policy intervention, is more complex. This research has shown that the decision to participate is a highly personal one based on several determining factors. Many of the interventions that will affect participation levels will be influenced from a national as opposed to a local level. To increase participation levels, national policies have to be made and pursued across a range of national agencies including:

- The Irish Sports Council
- Department of Tourism, Sport and Recreation
- Department of Education and Science
- Department of Health and Children
- Department of the Environment
- National Coaching and Training Centre
- Teacher training colleges
- Universities and Institutes of Technology
- National Youth Council.

However, the kinds of policies required to increase participation rates are difficult to legislate for, as they often have to deal with changing individual values. They also face other difficulties. Firstly, it can be difficult to produce results. Secondly, the results may be of a long-term rather than of a short-term nature. Thirdly, the results may also be difficult to quantify. Fourthly, the policy-makers may not get immediate recognition for any improvements in participation rates that are actually achieved. These are all issues that drive policy-makers who are under pressure to produce results. As a result, it is not surprising that the policy-makers tend to go for the easier options and have tackled primarily the short term and easily quantifiable issues of sports provision.

The data gathered from this research clearly show that tackling the generally low participation rates in sport by the many is the real challenge. If significant change is to occur, as is evidently needed, national agencies need to refocus and target policies aimed at increasing general participation rates by adolescents. There is a need for a fundamental shift in the way sport is delivered to Irish adolescents such that the notion of *sport for all who want it* becomes a reality.

To finish on a positive note, there have been some recent developments that deserve mention. The opening of the €63 million Waterworld in March 2003 bears testimony to government investment in sport that would have been unheard of in recent years. Secondly, the hosting of the Special Olympics World Games in June 2003 shows also a commitment by many Irish people to promote sport amongst a marginalised group within society. Let us hope that, in the future, the same level of commitment will be forthcoming for the development of youth sport.

BIBLIOGRAPHY

Ainsworth, J., 1978, "Women and Social Stratification: A Case of Intellectual Sexism", *American Journal of Sociology*, Vol. 78, No. 4.

Andrews, S. and O'Connor, C., 1990, *Space for Play*, Comhchairdeas, Dublin.

Alexandris, K. and Carroll, B., 1997, "Demographic Differences in the Perception of Constraints on Recreational Sports Participation: Results from a Study in Greece", *Leisure Studies*, Vol. 16, No. 2, pp. 107-126.

An Roinn Oideachais, 1996, *Liosta d'Iarbhunscoileanna*, Baile Atha Cliath, Stationery Office.

Archard, D., 1993, *Children: Rights and Childhood*, Routledge, London.

Aries, P., 1960, *Centuries of Childhood*, Penguin, Harmondsworth.

Armstrong, N., 1989, "Children are Fit but not Active", *Educational Health* 7, pp. 28-32.

Armstrong, N. and Biddle, S., 1990, "The Assessment of Children's Physical Activity Patterns", *Journal of Sport Sciences*, 8, 291.

Armstrong, N. and McManus, A., 1994a, "Physical Activity and the PE Curriculum", *British Journal of Physical Education*, Spring, Vol. 25, pp. 22-26.

Armstrong, N. and McManus, A., 1994b, "Children's Fitness and Physical Activity", *Physiotherapy in Sport*, 17, No. 3, pp. 6-10.

Backx, F., 1989, "Sports Injuries in School Aged Children", *American Journal of Sports Medicine*, Vol. 17, No. 2, pp. 234-239.

Ban, D., 1990, *Participation of Youth in Sports Organisations*, Paper presented at the fourth Congress of Yugoslav Pedagogics of Physical Culture, Bled, Yugoslavia.

Bandura, A., 1977, "Self-Efficacy: Towards a Unifying Theory of Behavioural Change", *Psychological Review*, 84, pp. 191-215.

Bandura, A., 1986, *A Social Foundation of Thought and Action: A Social Cognitive Theory*, Prentice Hall, New Jersey.

Bandura, A., 1994, "Social Cognitive Theory of Mass Communication" in Bryant, J. and Zillman, D. (eds.), *Media Effects: Advances in Theory and Research*, Hillsdale, New Jersey, pp. 61-90.

BARB Bulletin, August, 1987.

Beamish, R., 1990, "The Persistence of Inequality: An Analysis of Participation Patterns among Groups of High Performance Athletes", *International Review for the Sociology of Sport*, 25(2), pp. 143-153.

Beck, D. and Jones, M., 1973, cited in Ibrahim, H., 1991, *Leisure and Society — A Comparative Approach*, Brown Publishers, Indiana.

Beckers, T., 1989, "Does Sport Still Have a Future?", *Vrijetijd en Samenleving*, 7, pp. 83-94.

Bell, J., 1993, *Doing Your Research Project*, Open University Press, London.

Bennett, R., Duffy, A., Kalliam, D. and Martin, M., 1989, "Homophobia and Heterosexism in Sport and Physical Education: Why we Must Act Now", in *CAPERED Journal Times*, Vol. 51, No. 8.

Blair, S., Clark, D. and Cureton, K., 1989, "Exercise & Fitness in Childhood: Implications for a Lifetime of Health", *Perspectives in Exercise Science and Sports Medicine*, Vol. 2.

Bone, M., 1982, *The Youth Service and Similar Provision for Young People*, HMSO, London.

Bord Fáilte, 1996, *Annual Report*, Bord Fáilte, Dublin.

Bouchard, C., Shephard, R., Stephens, T., Sutton, J. and Mc Pherson, B., 1990, *Exercise, Fitness and Health*, Human Kinetics, Illinois.

Bourdieu, P., 1986, "The Forms of Capital", in J.G. Richardson (ed.), *Handbook of Theory and Research for the Sociology of Education*, New York, Greenwood Press.

Breen, R. and Whelan, C., 1996, *Social Mobility and Social Class in Ireland*, Gill and Macmillan, Dublin.

Brodie, J., 1992, *Physical Education into the 90s*, Paper presented at Liverpool Institute of Higher Education, proceedings published by SPRIG.

Browne, N., 1986, *Against the Tide*, Gill and Macmillan, Dublin.

Brustad, R., 1993a, "Who Will Go Out and Play? Parental and Psychological Influences on Children's Attraction to Physical Activity", *Paediatric Exercise Science*, 5, pp. 210-223.

Brustad, R., 1993b, "Youth in Sport: Psychological Considerations", *Research on Sports Psychology*, pp. 695-717.

Burton, D. and Martens, R., 1986, "Pinned by their Own Goals: An Exploratory Investigation into Why Kids Drop out of Wrestling", *Journal of Sport Psychology*, 8, pp. 183-197.

Busby, G., 1997, "Modelling Participation Motivation in Sport" in Kremer, J., Trew, K. and Ogle, S., 1997, *Young People's Involvement in Sport*, Routledge, London.

Butcher, J. and Hall, M., 1983, *Adolescent Girls' Participation in Physical Activity*, Edmonton Planning Services, Alberta.

Byrne, E., 1978, *Women and Education*, Tavistock, London.

Cairns, E., 1990, "The Relationship Between Perceived Self-competence and Attendance at Single Sex Secondary Schools", *British Journal of Educational Psychology*, 60, pp. 207-211.

Cahn, S., 1994, *Coming on Strong: Gender and Sexuality in Twentieth Century Women's Sport*, Free Press, New York.

Cale, L. and Harris, J., 1993, "Exercise Recommendations for Children and Young People", *Physical Education Review*, 16, No. 2, pp. 89-98.

Campbell, S., 1988, "Youth Sport in the United Kingdom", in Weiss, M.R. and Gould, D. (eds.), *Sport for Children and Youths*, Human Kinetics, Illinois, pp. 17-20.

Canada Fitness Survey, 1981, *Fitness and Lifestyle in Canada*, Government of Canada, Ottawa.

Carson, J., Burks, V. and Parke, R., 1993, "Parent-Child Physical Activity: Determinants and Consequences", in McDonald, K. (ed.), *Parent–Child Play*, SUNY Press, New York, pp. 197-220.

Caspersen, C., Powell, K., Christenson, G., 1995, "Physical Activity, Exercise and Physical Fitness. Definitions and Distinctions for Health Related Research", *Physical Health Report*, 100, pp. 126-131.

Central Council for Physical Recreation, 1960, *A Survey of Sport in Secondary Modern Schools*.

Central Statistics Office. For 1946, Statistical Abstracts of Ireland, 1946 table 9; for 1966, Census of Population of Ireland, 1966 vol. 1; for 1971, Census of Polulation,1971, vol. 1; for 1981, Census of Population, 1981, vol. 1; Demographic Information, 1999.

Chaney, D., 1996, *Lifestyles*, Routledge, London.

Christensen, J.E. and Youesting, D.R., 1978, "Social and Attitudinal Variants in High and Low Use of Outdoor Recreation Facilities", *Journal of Leisure Research*, Vol. 5, No. 2, pp. 20-34.

Clark, T.N. and Lipset, S.M., 1991, "Are Social Classes Dying?", *International Sociology*, Vol. 6, No. 4, pp. 397-410.

Clearing House, 1988, *Sport Participation in Norway*, Sports Information Bulletin, 13, 982.

Coakley, J., 1987, "Children and the Sport Socialisation Process" in Gould, D. and Weiss, M. (eds.), *Advances in Paediatric Sport Sciences, Vol. 2*, Human Kinetics, Illinois, pp. 43-60.

Coakley, J., 1996, *Sport in Society, Issues and Controversies*, 6th Edition, Mosby, St. Louis.

Coalter, F., 1993, "Sports Participation: Price or Priorities?", *Leisure Studies*, 12, pp. 171-182.

Coalter, F., Dowers, S. and Baxter, M., 1995, "The Impact of Social Class and Education on Sports Participation: Some Evidence from the General Household Survey" in Roberts, K. (ed.), *Leisure and Social Stratification*, Leisure Studies Association, pp. 59-73.

Cockerill, S. and Hardy, C., 1987, "The Attitudes of Fourth Year Girls Towards the Secondary School PE Curriculum", *Bulletin of Physical Education*, 23, No.1, Colorado Springs, pp. 6-12.

Coleman, J.S., 1961, *The Adolescent Society*, The Free Press, New York.

Coleman, J.S. (ed.), 1979, *The School Years*, Methuen, London.

Coleman, J.S. and Hendry, L., 1990, *The Nature of Adolescence*, 2nd ed., Routledge, London.

Collins, C. and Trenberth, L., 1994, *Sports Management in New Zealand, An Introduction*, Dunmore Press, Palmertown North.

Conger, J. and Petersen, A., 1984, *Adolescence and Youth*, Harper and Row, New York.

Connor, A., 1986, *How People Spend their Leisure Time*, Health Education Bureau.

Connor, S., 1997, *An Analysis of the Usage of Swimming Pools by Primary Schools in Waterford City*, Waterford Institute of Technology.

Connor, S., 1999, "Young People's Involvement in Sport in Waterford City", *Irish Journal of Psychology*, Summer.

Coolahan, J., 1985, *Irish Education History and Structure*, Kildare, Institute of Public Administration.

Coppersmith, S., 1967, *The Antecedents of Self-Esteem*, W.H. Freeman, San Francisco.

Corbin, C., 1980, cited in Ibrahim, H., 1991, *Leisure and Society: A Comparative Approach*, Brown Publishers, Indiana, p. 210.

Cresswell, J., 1998, *Qualitative Inquiry and Research Design*, Sage, California.

Crooks, T. and Mc Kiernan, J., 1984, *The Challenge of Change: Curriculum Development in Post Primary Schools 1970-1981*, IPA, Dublin.

Crowley, T., 1996, in *Irish Computer*, Vol. 24, No 1, Dublin, Computer Publication.

Crowley, L., 2000, *An Analysis of the Revised PE Curriculum for Irish Primary Schools*, BA Thesis, Waterford Institute of Technology.

Crum, B.J., 1991, *About the Sportification of Society*, Rijswijk, The Netherlands.

Darcy, M., 1985, *The Saints of Ireland*, Mercier Press, Cork.

Davis, J., 1990, *Youth and the Condition of Britain: Images of Adolescent Conflict*, Athlone Print, London.

Deem, R., 1986, *All Work and No Play? The Sociology of Women and Leisure*, Open University Press, Milton Keynes.

De Knop, P., Engstrom, L., Skirstad, B., Weiss, M., 1996, *World-Wide Trends in Youth Sport*, Human Kinetics, Illinois.

De Knop, P., Laporte, W., Van Meerbeek, R., Vanreusel, B., 1991, *Physical Fitness and Sport Participation among Flemish Youths*, IOS, Brussels.

Delamont, S., 1992, *Fieldwork in Educational Settings: Methods, Pitfalls and Perspectives*, Falmer Press, London.

Del Rey, 1978, "The Apologetic and Women in Sport", in *Women and Sport from Myth to Reality*, Lea and Febiger, Philadelphia.

Demo, D. and Savin-Williams, R., 1983, "Early Adolescent Self-Esteem as a Function of Social Class", *American Journal of Sociology*, Vol. 88, No. 4, pp. 763-774.

Dempsey, J., Kimiecik, J., Horn, T., 1993, "Parental Influence on Children's Moderate to Vigorous Physical Activity Participation: An Expectancy-Value Approach", *Paediatric Exercise Science*, 5, pp. 151-167.

Deenihan, J., 1991, *Physical Education Survey, Report on Physical Education in Irish Secondary Schools*, Dublin.

Department of Education, 1925, *Report of the Department of Education for the School Year 1924-1925 and the Financial and Administrative Year 1924-1925*, Stationery Office, Dublin.

Department of Education, 1928, *Report of Commission on Technical Education*, Stationery Office, Dublin.

Department of Education, 1988, *Physical Education Syllabus*, Government Publications, Dublin, Department of Education Report, 1924/5, pp. 24-25.

Department of Education, 1990, *Statistical Report, 1988-1989*, Government Publication, Dublin.

Department of Education Green Paper, 1992, *Education for a Changing World*, Stationery Office, Dublin.

Department of Education, 1995, *Charting Our Future, White Paper on Education*, Stationery Office, Dublin.

Department of Education, 1996, *A National Survey of Involvement in Sport and Physical Activity*, Dept. of Education, Dublin.

Department of Education, 1997, *Targeting Sporting Change in Ireland*, Stationery Office, Dublin.

Department of Education and Science, 1997, *Official Statistics*, Dublin, Stationery Office.

Department of Health, 1995, *A Health Promotion Strategy*, Stationery Office, Dublin.

Department of Health and Children, 1999, *Smoking and Drinking among Young People in Ireland*, Stationery Office, Dublin.

Department of Tourism, Sport and Recreation, 2000, *Strategic Planning for National Governing Bodies of Sport in Ireland*, Sports Council, Dublin.

Department of Sport and Recreation, Republic of South Africa, 1995, *Getting the Nation to Play*, RSA Government, Pretoria.

De Valera, Eamon, Speech to the Irish People quoted in Tim Pat Coogan, 1991, *Michael Collins*, Arrow Books, London.

Dietrich, K. and Heinemann, K. (eds.), 1989, *The Nonsporting Sport*, Schorndorf, Germany.

Diller, A. and Houston, B., 1983, "Women's Physical Education: A Gender Sensitive Perspective", published in *Women, Philosophy and Sport: A Collection of New Essays*, The Scarecrow Press, London.

Doorly, P. and Hynes, M., 1995, "Illegal Sales of Cigarettes to Children in Northeast Dublin", *Irish Medical Journal*, Vol. 88, No. 4, pp. 130-131.

Drummy, V.J. and Watson, A.W.S., 1992, *Activity and Life — Style Characteristics of Irish School Children Ages 10-13*, Dept. of Education, Dublin, pp. 3-13.

Duffy, P., 1987, *Conference Papers and Working Party Recommendation to the Minister for Sport*, Cospóir, Dublin, pp. 53-65.

Duffy, P. and Sleap, M., 1982, "Factors Affecting Active Participation in Sport by the Working Class" in *International Review of Sport Sociology*, Vol. 1, No. 17.

Dunning, E. (ed.), 1983, *The Sociology of Sport*, Frank Cass, London.

Duquin, M., 1978, "The Androgynous Advantage", in *Women and Sport: From Myth to Reality*, Lea and Febiger, Philadelphia.

Ebbeck, V. and Weiss, M., 1992, *Antecedents of Children's Self Esteem: An Examination of Perceived Competence and Effect on Sport*, Paper presented at the meeting of the Association for the Advancement of Applied Sports Psychology.

Eccles, J.S. and Harold, R., 1991, "Gender Differences in Sport Involvement: Applying the Eccles Expectancy Value Model", *Journal of Applied Sport Psychology*, 3, pp. 7-35.

Eisner, G. and Turner, D., 1983, "Myth and Reality: Social Mobility of the American Olympic Athletes", *International Review for the Sociology of Sport*, Vol. 27, No. 2, pp. 165-183.

Elkind, D., 1967, "Egocentrism in Adolescence", *Child Development*, 38, pp. 1025-34.

Emmett, I., 1971, *Youth and Leisure in an Urban Sprawl*, Manchester University Press, Manchester.

Epstein, J. (ed.), 1998, *Youth Culture, Identity in a Post-Modern World*, Blackwell Publishers, Oxford.

Eurostat, 1992, *Demographic Statistics, 1991*, Eurostat.

Farrell, J., 1999, *An Investigation into the Provision of Sporting Programmes by Local Councils in Ireland with A Case Study of North Dublin Community*, M.Sc. Thesis, University of Leicester.

Felshin, J., 1974, "The Social View", published in *The American Woman in Sport*, Addison Wesley Publishing.

Feltz, D.L., 1978, "Athletes in the Status System of Female Adolescents", *Review of Sport and Leisure*, Vol. 3, No. 1, Fall.

Fitzclarence, L. and Tinning, R., 1992, "Post-Modern Youth Culture and the Crisis in Australian Secondary Physical Education", *Quest*, Vol. 44, No. 3, pp. 287-304.

Flanagan, P., 2002, *An Examination of the Relationship between Lung Function and Aerobic Capacity in People with Asthma*, Unpublished MSc Thesis, Institute of Technology, Tralee.

Foster, A., 1984, *Fitness Patterns of Irish Rural Adults*, BA thesis, Waterford Regional Technical College.

Fox, K., Corbin, C. and Couldry, W., 1985, "Female Physical Estimation and Attraction to Physical Activity", *Journal of Sports Psychology*, 7, pp. 125-136.

Freedson, P. and Evenson, S, 1991, "Family Aggregation in Physical Activity", *Research Quarterly for Exercise and Sport*, 62, pp. 384-389.

Frith, S., 1978, *The Sociology of Rock*, Constable Press, London.

GAA Strategic Review, 2002, *Enhancing Community Identity*, Costar Associates, Dublin

Gaines, D., 1994, "Suicidal Tendencies: Kurt Cobain did not Die for You", *Rolling Stone*, June 2, pp. 59-61.

Gallagher, B., 1997, *Golf Courses and Golfing Establishment — Development and Impact in Ireland*, PhD thesis, University of Dublin.

Galvin, C.J., 1983, *Leisure Activity Among School Going Adolescents in a Midlands Town*, BA Thesis, Thomond College of Education.

Gavron, H., 1966, *The Captive Wife*, Routledge, London.

Gibbons, L., 1996, *Transformations in Irish Culture*, Cork University Press, Cork.

Giddens, A., 1992, *Human Societies: A Reader*, Polity Press, Cambridge.

Giddens, A., 1973, *The Class Structure of the Advanced Societies*, Hutchinson, London.

Giddens, A., 1994, *Sociology*, Polity Press, Cambridge.

Girls on Television, Washington DC, National Commission on Working Women of Wider Opportunities for Women

Goldthorpe, J., 1969, *The Affluent Workers in the Class Structure*, University Press, Cambridge.

Goldthorpe, J., 1992, *Revised Class Schema, 1992*, JUSST Working Paper, no.13, Nuffield College and SCPR.

Goldthorpe, J.H. and Marshall, G., 1992, "The Promising Future of Class Analysis: A Response to Recent Critiques", *Sociology*, Vol. 26, No. 3, pp. 381-400.

Gottlieb, N., Chen, M., 1985, "Socio-Cultural Correlates of Childhood Sporting Activities: Their Implications for Heart Health", *Social Science in Medicine*, Vol. 21, No. 5, pp. 533-539.

Granleese, J., Turner, I. and Trew, K., 1989, "Teachers' and Boys' and Girls' Perception of Competence in the Primary School: The Importance of Physical Competence", *British Journal of Educational Psychology*, 59, pp. 31-37.

Gratton, C. and Taylor, P., 1988, *Sport and Recreation, An Economic Analysis*, Arrowsmith Ltd., Bristol.

Greendorfer, S., 1983, "Shaping the Female Athlete: The Impact of the Family" in Boutilier, M., *The Sporting Woman*, Human Kinetics, Illinois.

Greendorfer, S. and Ewing, M., 1994, "Race and Gender Differences in Children's Socialisation into Sport", *Research Quarterly for Exercise and Sport*, 52, pp. 301-310.

Greendorfer, S. and Lewko, J., 1988, *Children's Socialisation into Sport: a Conceptual and Empirical Analysis*, Paper from the World Congress of Sociology.

Griffin, P. and Genasci, J., 1990, "Addressing Homophobia in Physical Education: Responsibilities for Teachers and Researchers" in Messner, M. (ed.), *Sport, Men and the Gender Order*, Human Kinetics, Illinois.

Griffin, P., 1993a, "Homophobia in Sport: Addressing the Needs of Lesbian and Gay High School Athletes" in *High School Journal (Chapel Hill)*, Vol. 75.

Griffin, P., 1993b, "Homophobia in Women's Sport: The Fear that Divides Us", in Cohen, G. (ed.), *Women in Sport: Issues and Controversies*, Sage, California.

Griffin, P., 1993c, *What's a Nice Girl Like You Doing in a Profession Like This?* Quest Monograph, pp. 96-101.

Grube, P., Joel, M. and Morgan, M., 1986, *Smoking, Drinking and Drug Use among Post-Primary School Pupils*, Paper No. 132, Economic and Social Research Institute, Dublin.

Grube, P., Joel, M. and Morgan, M., 1990, *The Development and Maintenance of Smoking, Drinking and Other Drug Use among Dublin Post-Primary School Pupils*, Paper No. 148, Economic and Social Research Institute, Dublin.

Grube, P., Joel, M. and Morgan, M., 1994, *Drinking among Post-Primary School Pupils*, Paper No. 164, Economic and Social Research Institute, Dublin.

Gruneau, R., 1975, "Sport, Social Differientiation and Social Inequality" in Bell, D.W. and Loy, J. (eds.), *Sport and Social Order: Contributions to the Sociology of Sport*, Addison-Wesley, Reading, pp. 117-184.

Gunter, B and Mc Aleer, J., 1997, *Children and Television*, 2nd Edition, Routledge, London.

Hange, A., 1973, "The Influence of the Family on Female Sports Participation" in *Physical Activity: Human Growth and Development*, Academic Press, New York.

Haralambos, J. and Holborn P., 1995, *Sociology, Themes and Perspectives*, Collins, New York.

Hargreaves, J., 1980, *Sport and Hegemony*, paper presented at Sport, Culture and Ideology Conference 1980, British Sports Council, London.

Hargreaves, J., 1985, "Playing Like Gentlemen While Behaving like Ladies: Contradictory Features of the Formative Years of Women's Sport", *The British Journal of Sports History*, Vol. 2, No. 1, pp. 40-52.

Hargreaves, J., 1986, *Sport, Power and Culture*, Polity Press, London.

Hargreaves, J., 1994, *Sporting Females, Critical Issues in the History and Sociology of Women's Sports*, Routledge, London.

Harris, D., 1971, "The Sportswoman in Our Society", in DGWS Research Reports, *Women in Sport*, American Association for Health, Education and Recreation, Washington DC, pp. 1-4.

Harter, S., 1981, *A Model of Intrinsic Mastery Motivation in Children: Individual Differences and Development Change*, Minnesota Symposium on Child Psychology, Vol. 14, pp. 215-255.

Harter, S., 1982, "The Perceived Competence Scale for Children", in *Child Development*, Vol. 53, pp. 87-97.

Haywood, K., 1991, "The Role of Physical Education in the Development of Active Lifestyles", *Research Quarterly for Exercise and Sport*, 62, pp. 151-156.

Health Promotion Unit, 1994, S*moking and Drinking Among Young People*, Dept. of Health, Dublin.

Health Promotion Unit, 1996, *A National Survey of Involvement in Sport and Physical Activity,* Health Promotion Unit, Dublin.

Hellstedt, J., 1990, "Early Adolescent Perceptions of Parental Pressure in the Sport Environment", in *Journal of Sport Behaviour*, Vol. 13, No. 3, pp. 135-144.

Hendry, L., 1978, *School, Sport and Leisure*, Lepus Books, London.

Hendry, L., Shucksmith, J., Love, J. and Glendinning, A., 1993, *Young People's Leisure and Lifestyle*, Routledge, London.

Henley Centre, 1987, "Capitalising on Social Change", *Leisure Futures*, March.

Hogan, G., 1998, "Juvenile Crime in Waterford City", article in *Waterford News and Star*, February.

Holton, R. and Turner, B., 1994, "Debate and Pseudo-Debate in Class Analysis, Some Unpromising Aspects of Goldthorpe and Marshall's Defence", *Sociology*, 28, pp. 799-804.

Horn, T.S. and Hasbrook, C.A., 1996, "Informational Components Influencing Children's Perceptions of their Physical Competencies" in Weiss, M.R. and Gould, D. (eds.), *Sport for Children and Youths*, 1984 Olympics Congress Proceedings, Vol. 10, Human Kinetics, Illinois, pp. 89-102.

Horn, T.S., Gleen, S.D. and Wentzell, A.B., 1993, "Sources of Information Underlying Personal Ability Judgements in High School Athletes", *Paediatric Exercise Science*, 5, pp. 263-274.

Houlihan, G., 1998, *Factors Impacting on Local Authority Leisure Centre Usage*, Paper at ILAM Ireland Conference.

Howard, D. and Crampton, J., 1984, "Who are the Consumers of Public Park and Recreation Services?" *Journal of Park and Recreation Administration*, Vol. 2, No. 3, pp. 33-48.

Howard, S. (ed.), 1998, *Wired up, Young People and the Electronic Media*, UCL Press, London.

Howarth, K., 1988, "Women and Sport: Issues of Relevance to the Female Primary School Teacher", *British Journal of Physical Education*, Vol. 18, No. 6, pp. 269-270.

Hussey, G., 1995, *Ireland Today, Anatomy of a Changing State*, Penguin Books, London.

Ibrahim, H., 1991, *Leisure and Society: A Comparative Approach*, Brown Publishers, Indiana.

Ilich, I., 1986, *Deschooling Society*, Penguin, Harmondsworth.

Incantalupo, P., 1994, *The Portrayal of Women in Sport Advertising in Two Women's Sports Magazines*, Microform Publications, Oregon.

Irish Basketball Association, 1998, *Annual Report, 1997*, Dublin.

Irish Times Supplement, *Education and Living*, p. 3, 9 December 1997.

Iso-Ahola, S., 1994, "Leisure, Lifestyle and Health", in *Leisure and Mental Health*, Family Development Resources, Park City Utah, pp. 420-460.

Jackson, E. and Dunn, E., 1988, "Integrating Ceasing Participation with other Aspects of Leisure Behaviour", *Journal of Leisure Research*, 20, pp. 31-45.

Jones, G., 1988, "Integrating Process and Structure in the Concept of Youth: A Case for Secondary Analysis", *The Sociology Review*, Vol. 36, No. 4, pp. 706-32.

Kane, E., 1997, *Doing Your Own Research*, Boyars Publishers, London.

Kaprio, J., Koskenvou, M. and Sarns, S., 1981, "Cigarette Smoking, Use of Alcohol and Leisure Time Activity among Same Sexed Adult Male Twins", *Progress in Clinical and Biological Research*, Vol. 69, pp. 37-47.

Kay, T. and Jackson, G., 1991, "Leisure Despite Constraints: the Impact of Leisure Constraints on Leisure Participation", *Journal of Leisure Research*, 23, pp. 301-313.

Kenyon, G.S., 1966, "The Significance of Physical Activity as a Function of Age, Sex, Education and Socio-Economic Status of Northern United States Adults", *International Review of Sports Sociology*, No. 6, pp. 41-57.

Kenyon, G.S. and McPherson, B.D., 1973, "Becoming Involved in Physical Activity and Sport: A Process of Socialisation" in *Physical Activity: Human Growth and Development*, Academic Press, New York, pp. 24-36.

Kephart, W., 1982, *Extraordinary Groups: the Sociology of Unconventional Lifestyles*, 2nd Edition, St. Martin's Press, New York.

Kimiecik, J., Allison, M. and Duda, J., 1986, "Performance Satisfaction, Perceived Competence and Game Outcome: The Competitive Experience of Boys' Youth Club", *International Journal of Sport Psychology*, 17, pp. 255-268.

Kirk, D. and Tinning, R., 1990, *Physical Education, Curriculum and Culture, Critical Issues in the Contemporary Crisis*, Falmer Press, London.

Kirshnit, C., Ham, M. and Richards, M., 1989, "The Sporting Life: Athletic Activities During Early Adolescence", *Journal of Youth and Adolescence*, Vol. 18, No. 6, pp. 601-615.

Kohr, R., 1988, "The Influence of Race, Class and Gender on Self-Esteem of Fifth, Eighth and Eleventh Grade Students in Pennsylvania Schools", *Journal of Negro Education*, Vol. 57, No. 4, pp. 467-481.

Kremer, J., Trew, K. and Ogle, S., 1997, *Young People's Involvement in Sport*, Routledge, London.

Lamon, A., 1977, "Some Aspects of Social Status, Culture and Promotion Factors of the Family in Relation to Sports Practice", in *International Review of Sport Sociology*, Vol. 4, No. 12, pp. 5-13.

Landers, D.M. and Luschen, G., 1970, "Sibling Sex Status and Ordinal Position Effects on the Sports Participation of Females", in *Women Athletes in Contemporary Society*, Arno Press, New York.

Landers, D., 1970, "Psychological Femininity and the Prospective Female Physical Educator", *Research Quarterly for Exercise & Fitness*, pp. 164-170.

Larson, R., 1995, "Variations of Experience in Informal and Formal Sports", *Research Quarterly for Exercise and Sport*, 55.

Leaman, O., 1984, *Sit on the Sidelines and Watch the Boys Play: Sex Differentiation in Physical Education*, Longman, London.

Lenskyj, H., 1990, *Out of Bounds: Women, Sport and Sexuality*, Women's Press, Toronto.

Lewko, J. and Greendorfer, S., 1988, "Family Influences in Sport Socialisation of Children and Adolescents" in Smoll et al. (eds.), *Children in Sport*, Human Kinetics, Illinois, pp. 287-300.

Lounsbury, J. and Hoopes, L., 1988, "Five Year Stability of Leisure Activity and Motivation Factors", *Journal of Leisure Research*, 20, pp. 31-45.

Luschen, G., 1969, "Social Stratification and Social Mobility Amongst Young Sportsmen" in Loy, J. and Kenyon, G. (eds.), *Sport, Culture and Society: A Reader on the Sociology of Sport*, Macmillan, Toronto, pp. 258-276.

Luschen, G., 1970, "Social Stratification and Mobility among Young German Sportsmen", in Dunning, E. (ed.), *The Sociology of Sport*, Cass, London, pp. 230-243.

Lynch, K., 1989, *The Hidden Curriculum*, The Falmer Press, London.

McArt, P. and Campbell, D. (eds.), 1997, *Irish Almanac: Yearbook of Facts*, Artcam Publishing, Derry.

McCrone, K.E., 1988, *Sport and the Physical Emancipation of English Women, 1870-1914*, Routledge, London.

McIntosh, P.C., 1959, *PE in England since 1900*, Bell Publishers, London.

McKay, J. and Pearson, K., 1986, "Socio-Demographic Characteristics of Elite Australian Athletes: An Exploratory Case Study" in Mangan, J. and Small, R. (eds.) *Sport, Culture and Society*, E. and F.N. Spon, New York, pp. 298-305.

McKiddle, B. and Maynard, I., 1997, "Perceived Competence of School-children in Physical Education", *Journal of Teaching of Physical Education*, No. 16, 1997, Human Kinetics Publishers, Illinois, pp. 324-339.

McPherson, B.D., Curtis, J.E. and Loy, J.W., 1989, *The Social Significance of Sport*, Human Kinetics, Illinois.

Malumphy, T., 1970, "The College Woman Athlete, Questions and Tentative Answers", published in *Quest*.

Mangan, J.A., 1983, "Grammar Schools and the Games Ethic in Victorian and Edwardian Eras", *Albion*, Vol. 15, No. 4, pp. 313-335.

Manual for the Self-Perception Profile for Children, 1982, Sports Council (UK).

Mason, V., 1995, *Young People and Sport in England, 1994, a National Study*, Sports Council, London.

Mathes, S., 1978, "Body Image and Sex Stereotyping", in *Women and Sport: From Myth to Reality*, Lea and Febiger, Philadelphia.

Melcher, N. and Sage, G.,1996, "The Relationship between Parental Attitude Towards Physical Activity and the Attitudes and Motor Development of their Daughters", *International Review of Sport Sociology*, Vol. 32, No. 2.

Messner, M., 1988, "Sports and Male Domination: The Female Athlete as Contested Ideological Terrain", *Sociology of Sport Journal*, pp. 197-211.

Metheny, E., 1965, "Symbolic Forms of Movement, The Feminine Image in Sports" in *Connotations of Movement in Sport and Dance*, pp 43-56.

Michener, J., 1976, *Sports in America*, Random House, New York.

Miller Lite, 1983, *Report on American Attitudes to Sport*, Miller Brewing Company, Milwaukee.

Moleres, F., 1998, "All Work and No Play", *The Sunday Times*, London. , pp. 32-40.

Montoye, H., Kemper, H., Sarris, W., Washburn, R., 1996, *Measuring Physical Activity and Energy Expenditure*, Human Kinetics, Illinois.

Moore, L., Lombardi, D., White, M., Campbell, J, Oliveira, S., Ellison, R, "Influence of Parent's Physical Activity Levels on the Activity Levels of Young Children". *Journal of Paediatrics*, Vol. 118, No. 2, pp. 215-219.

Moss, H.A. and Kagan, J., 1961, "Stability of Achievement and Recognition Seeking Behaviours from Early Childhood", *Journal of Abnormal and Social Psychology*, pp. 504-513.

Mulligan, J., 1999, *Physical Activity Patterns among Irish Male Junior Certificate Students*, MA thesis, Waterford Institute of Technology.

Nicholls, J., 1984, "Conceptions of Ability, Subjective Experience, Task Choice and Performance", *Psychological Review*, 91, pp. 328-346.

Nielson, L., 1983, "Putting Away the Pom-Poms: An Educational Psychologist's View of Females in Sport" in *Women, Philosophy and Sport, A Collection of New Essays*, The Scarecrow Press, London, pp. 293-294.

Noonan, O. and O'Malley, S., 1987, *The Level of Participation in Physical Activities by Past Pupils of Crescent College Comprehensive Limerick*, PEAI, Limerick.

Northern Ireland Fitness Survey, 1989, *Northern Ireland Health and Fitness Survey*, Queens University of Belfast.

O'Brien, S. and Ford, R., 1989, "Can We at Last Say Goodbye to Social Class?" *Journal of the Market Research Society*, Vol. 30, No. 3, pp. 289-329.

O'Connor, J., 1986, *The Fitness Levels of the Irish Population*, Health Education Bureau, Dublin.

O'Connor, J. and Daly, M., 1983, *The West Limerick Study*, Social Research Centre, Limerick.

O'Dea, P., 1994, *A Class of our Own: Conversations about Class in Ireland*, New Island Books, Dublin.

Offe, C., 1985, "Work: The Key Sociological Category", in Keane, J. (ed.), *Disorganised Capitalism*, Polity Press, Cambridge.

Ogle, S., 1994, *The Assessment of Adult Participation in Sport and Physical Recreation in Northern Ireland 1983-1993*, Belfast, Sports Council for Northern Ireland.

Ogle, S., 1997, "International Policy Perspectives", in Kremer, J., Trew, K. and Ogle, S., 1997, *Young People's Involvement in Sport*, Routledge, London.

O'Reilly, 2000, "The Realities of Coaching Teenagers", paper given at national coaching seminar organised by the Football Association of Ireland, Dublin, January 2000.

Orthner, D., 1985, *Conflict and Leisure Interaction in Families* cited in Gunter, B. and Lanham, M. (eds.), 1991, *Transition to Leisure: Conceptual and Human Issues*, Brown Publishers.

O'Toole, F., 1997, *The Ex-Isle of Erin*, New Island Books, Dublin.

Pahl, R.E., 1989, "Is the Emperor Naked? Some Comments on the Adequacy of Sociological Theory in Urban and Rural and Regional Research", *International Journal of Urban and Regional Research*, 15, pp. 127-129.

Parker, S., 1971, *The Future of Work and Leisure*, Paladin, London.

Parry, N. and Johnson, D., 1974, *Leisure and Social Structure*, London, Science Research Council.

Parsons, J., Adler, T. and Kaczala, C, 1982, "Socialisation of Achievement Attitudes and Beliefs: Parental Influences", *Child Development*, 53, pp. 310-321.

Pellett, T. and Ignico, A., 1993, "The Relationship between Children's and Parents' Stereotyping of Physical Activities", *Perceptual and Motor Skills*, Vol. 3, Part 2.

Perusse, L., Tremblay, A., LeBlanc, C., Bouchard, C., 1989, "Genetic and Environmental Influences on Levels of Habitual Physical Activity and Exercise Participation", *American Journal of Epidemiology*, Vol. 129, No. 5, pp. 1012-1022.

Petersen, D. and Gardener, M., 1989, *Handbook on Adolescent Development*, Maryland Department of Health and Mental Hygiene.

Phillips, D., 1987, "Socialisation of Perceived Academic Competence among Highly Competent Children", *Child Development*, 58, pp. 1308-1320.

Physical Education Association, 1987, *Physical Education in School*, Ling Publishing House, London.

Pittman, K., 1991, *A New Vision, Promoting Youth Development*, Testimony before the House Select Committee on Children, Youth and Families, Washington DC, 30 September 1991.

Pollak, A., 1998, "Is our Education System Biased against Poor People?", *Irish Independent*, Dublin.

Postman, N., 1985, *The Disappearance of Childhood*, Comet, London.

Power, T. and Woolger, C., 1994, "Parenting Practices and Age Group Swimmers — A Correlational Study" in *Research Quarterly for Exercise and Sport*, Vol. 65, No. 1, pp. 59-66.

Pronger, B., 1994, "Gay Jocks: A Phenomenology of Gay Men in Athletics", in Messner, M. (ed.), *Women in Sports: Interdisciplinary Perspectives*, Brown, Indiana, pp. 43-56.

Purdy, D., Eitzen, D. and Haufler, R., 1982, "Are Athletes also Students? The Educational Attainment of College Athletes", *Social Problem*, Vol. 29, No. 4, pp. 438-448.

Raymore, T., Godbey, M. and Crawford, D., 1994, "Self Esteem, Gender and Socio-Economic Status — Their Relation to Perceptions of Constraints on Leisure among Adolescents", *Journal of Leisure Research*, Vol. 26, No. 2, pp. 99-118.

Renson, R., 1976, *Social Status Symbolism of Sport Stratification*, Hermes, 10, Human Kinetics, Illinois, pp. 433-443.

Report of Commission on Technical Education, 1927, Stationery Office, Dublin.

Research Unit in Health and Behavioural Change, 1989, *Changing the Public Health*, Wiley, Chichester.

Richman, C., Clark, M. and Brown, K., 1985, "General and Specific Self-Esteem in Late Adolescent Students", *Adolescence*, Vol. 20, No. 79, pp. 555-556.

Riess, S.A., 1990, "Professional Sports as an Avenue of Social Mobility in America: Some Myths and Realities" in Kirk, D.G. and Stark, G.D. (eds.), *Essays on Sport History and Sport Mythology*, A. and M. Press, Texas.

Roberts, K., 1978, *Contemporary Society and the Growth of Leisure*, Longman, London.

Roberts, K. and Kamphorst, T., 1990, *Trends in Sport: A Multi-National Perspective*, Giordano Bruno Culembourg, Voorthuizen.

Roberts, K. and Parsell, G., 1991, "Young People's Sources and Levels of Income and Patterns of Consumption in Britain in the late 80s", *Youth and Policy*, 35, pp. 20-25.

Rosenberg, M., 1989, *Society and the Adolescent Self Image*, Princeton University Press, New Jersey.

Ross, J., Dotson, C., Gilbert, G., 1985, "Are Kids Getting Appropriate Activity?" *Journal of Physical Education, Recreation and Dance*, 56, pp. 82-85.

Ross, J., Pate, R., Carpersen, C., Damberg, C., Svilar, M., 1987, "Home and Community in Children's Exercise Habits", *Journal of Physical Education Recreation and Dance*, November–December, pp. 85-92.

Rosseau, J.J., 1860, *Emile*, Penguin Press, London.

Rotella, R. and Murray, M., 1991, "Homophobia, the World of Sport and Sport Psychology Consulting", in *Sport Psychologist*, Vol. V, No. IV, December 1991.

Rusidill, M., 1990, "Influence of Perceived Competence and Causal Dimension Orientation on Expectation, Persistence and Performance during Perceived Failure", *Research Quarterly for Exercise and Sport*, 60, pp. 166-175.

Sage, G., 1990, *Power and Ideology in American Sport: A Critical Perspective*, Human Kinetics, Illinois.

Sallis, J., Alcaraz, J., McKenzie, T., Hovell, M., Kolody, B., Nader, P., 1992, "Parental Behaviour in Relation to Physical Activity and Fitness in 9-Year-Old Children", *American Journal of Diseases in Children*, 146, pp. 1383-1388.

Sallis, J., Haskell, W., Fortmann, S., Vranizan, K., Taylor, C. and Soloman, D., 1986, "Predicators of Adoption and Maintenance of Physical Activity in a Community Sample", *Preventative Medical Journal*, Vol. 15, pp. 331-341.

Sallis, J.F., Patterson, T., McKenzie, T. and Nader, P., 1988, "Family Variables and Physical Activity in Pre-school Children", *Journal of Developmental and Behavioural Paediatrics*, 9, pp. 57-61.

Sallis, J. and Patrick, K., 1994, *Paediatric Exercise Science*, Vol. 6, pp. 301-314.

Scarr, S., 1966, "Genetic Factors in Activity Motivation", *Child Development*, 37, pp. 663-671.

Scott, D. and Willits, F., 1989, "Adolescents and Leisure Patterns: A 37-Year Follow-Up Study", *Leisure Sciences*, 11, pp. 323-335.

Scott, J., 1974, "Men and Women in Sport: The Manhood Myth", in *Issues in Physical Education and Sport*, National Press Books, California.

Seppanean, P., 1982, "Sports Clubs and Parents as Socialising Agents in Sport", in *International Review for the Sociology of Sport*, 17, pp. 79-90.

Sewart, J.J, 1987, "The Commodification of Sport", *International Review for the Sociology of Sport*, No. 22, pp. 171-191.

Shropshire, J., Carroll, B., 1997, "Family Variables and Children's Physical Activity: Influence of Parental Exercise and Socio-Economic Status", *Sport, Education and Society*, Vol. 2, No. 1, pp. 95-116.

Silbereisen, R., Noack, P. and von Eye, E., 1992, "Adolescents' Development of Romantic Friendship and Change in Favourite Leisure Contexts", *Journal of Adolescent Research*, Vol. 7, No. 1, pp. 80-93.

Simons-Morton, B.G., O'Hara, N.M., Parcel, G.S. and Pate, R.R., 1988, "Health-Related Physical Fitness in Childhood: Status and Recommendations", *Annual Review of Public Health*, No. 9, pp. 403-425.

Sleap, M. and Warburton, P., 1992, "Physical Activity Levels of 5-11 Year Old Children in England as Determined by Direct Observation", *Research Quarterly for Exercise and Sport*, 63, pp. 238-245.

Smeets, P., 1990, "Indoor Swimming Pools, Arrangements, Visits and Exploitation", *Sociall-Culturele Berichten*, 16, pp.1-10.

Smith, D.H. and Harrison, J.M., 1987, *Why People Recreate: an Overview of Research*, Life Enhancement Publications, Illinois.

Smoll, F. and Smith, R., 1996, *Children and Youth in Sport*, Brown and Benchmark, Chicago.

Snyder, E.E. and Kivlin, J.E., 1975, "A Study of Women Athletes and Aspects of the Feminine Role, Psychological Well Being and Body Image", in *Women Athletes in Contemporary Society*, Arno Press, New York.

Sports Council, 1982, *Sport in the Community, the Next Ten Years*, The Sports Council, London.

Sports Council, 1991, *A Digest of Sports Statistics for the UK*, The Sports Council, London.

Starosta, W., 1967, "Some Data Concerning Social Characteristics of Figure Skaters", *International Review of Sports Sociology*, 2, pp. 165-178.

Steenland, S., 1988, *Growing Up in Prime Time: An Analysis of Adolescent Television Viewing Patterns*, Sage, California.

Stensaasen, S., 1982, "A Co-ordinated Comparative Study of Sports Involvement among Scandinavian Youngsters", *Scandinavian Journal of Sport Sciences*, 1, pp. 17-25.

Stipek, D. and McIver, D., 1989, "Developmental Change in Children's Assessment of Intellectual Competence", *Child Development*, 60, pp. 521-538.

Strasburger, V., 1995, *Adolescents and the Media: Medical and Psychological Impact*, Sage, California.

Straus, M., Gellis, R. and Steinmets, S., 1980, cited in Ibrahim, H., 1991, *Leisure and Society: A Comparative Approach*, Brown Publishers, New York.

Sutherland, A., 1992, *Physical Education and Games in Post-Primary Schools in 1991*, Sports Council Northern Ireland, Belfast.

Sutton-Smith, B., Rosenberg, B.G. and Morgan, E.E., 1963, "The Development of Sex Differences in Play Choices during Preadolescence", *Journal of Child Development*, pp. 119-126.

Szali, A. (ed.), 1973, *The Use of Time, Daily Activities of Urban and Suburban Populations in Twelve Countries*, The Hague.

Talbot, M.J., 1978, *The Household Woman*, published in Yorkshire and Humberside Council for Sport and Recreation Conference Report on Urban Deprivation and the Role of Sport and Recreation.

Talbot, M., 1979, *Women and Leisure*, Sports Council, London.

Taylor, A., 1990, *To School through the Fields*, Brandon Books, Kerry.

Teachers Union of Ireland, 1997, Several quotes in *The Irish Times* and *Irish Independent* from representatives of the Teachers Unions at their Annual congresses, Easter 1997.

Telford, K., 1998, "The American Olympic Athletes", *International Review of the Sociology of Sport*, Vol. 27, No. 2, pp. 165-73.

The Leaflet, Vol. 45, No. 6, 1946.

Thirlaway, K. and Benton, D., 1993, "Physical Activity in Primary and Secondary School Children in West Glamorgan", *Health Education Journal*, Vol. 52, No. 1, pp. 37-41.

Tomlinson, P., 1995, *Sociology of Leisure*, E & F. Spon, London.

UNICEF, 1996, *Convention on the Rights of the Child*, UNICEF, Dublin.

Van Wersch, A., 1990, *A Social-Psychological Model of Interest in Physical Education: Age, Gender and School Type Differences*, PhD Thesis, Queens University, Belfast.

Van Wersch, A., 1997, "Individual Differences and Intrinsic Motivations for Sport Participation" in Kremer, J., Trew, K. and Ogle, S., *Young People's Involvement in Sport*, Routledge, London.

Veal, A.J., 1993, "The Concept of Lifestyle, A Review", in *Leisure Studies*, 12, E. & F.N. Spon, London.

Veal, A.J., 1994, *Leisure Policy and Planning*, Longman, London.

Verschuur, R. and Kemper, H., 1985, "The Pattern of Physical Daily Activity", *Medicine Sport Science*, 20, pp. 169-186.

Wales Sports Council, 1987, *Exercise for Health-Related Fitness in Wales*, Heartbeat Report, No. 23.

Watson, A.W.S., 1990a, *Tests of Physical Fitness on Children from National Schools*, Research Report, No.4, Cospóir Research Committee, Dublin.

Watson, A.W.S., 1990b, *Aspects of Health-Related Fitness of Second Level Children: Physical Fitness, Body Mechanics and Knowledge of Health and Lifestyle*, Research Report, No.6, Cospóir Research Committee, Dublin.

Watson, A.W.S., 1996, *Physical Fitness and Athletic Performance*, 2nd edition, Longman Group, London.

Watson, A.W.S., 2000, "Worry about the Fitness Levels of Irish Teenagers", *Irish Independent*, January.

Weiss, M. and Bredemeier, B., 1983, "Developmental Sport Psychology: A Theoretical Perspective for Studying Children in Sport", *Journal of Sport Psychology*, 7, pp. 75-91.

Weiss, M. and Chaumeton, N., 1992, "Motivation Orientation in Sport" in T.S. Horn (ed.), *Advances in Sport Psychology*, Human Kinetics, Illinois, pp. 61-99.

Weiss, M. and Hayashi, C., 1995, "All in the Family: Parent Child Influence in Competitive Youth Gymnastics", *Paediatric Exercise Science*, 7, pp. 36-48.

Weiss, M.R. and Gould, D. (eds.), 1984, *Sport for Children and Youths*, Olympics Congress Proceedings, Vol. 10, Human Kinetics, Illinois, pp. 89-102.

Weiss, M.R. and Horn, T.S., 1990, "The Relationship Between Children's Accuracy Estimates of their Physical Competence and Achievement-Related Characteristics", *Research Quarterly for Exercise and Sport*, 61, pp. 250-258.

Weiss, M.R., Bredemeier, B.J. and Shewchuk, 1986, "The Dynamics of Perceived Competence, Perceived Control and Motivational Orientation in Youth Sport", *Paediatric Exercise Science*, Vol. 6, No. 4, pp. 302-312.

West, J., 1965, *The Young Offender*, Penguin, Harmondsworth.

West, P., 1988, "Inequalities? Social Class Differences in Health in British Youths", *Social Science and Medicine*, Vol. 27, No. 4, pp. 291-296.

White, A. and Coakley, J., 1986, *Making Decisions, The Response of Young People in the Medway Towns to the 'Ever Thought of Sport' Campaign*, Greater London and the South East Region Sports Council, London.

Willerman, L., 1973, "Activity Levels and Hyperactivity in Twins", *Child Development*, 4, pp. 288-293.

Williams, A., 1993, "Who Cares about Girls? Equality, Physical Education and the Primary School", in Evans, J. (ed.), *Equality, Education and Physical Education*, Falmer Press, London, pp. 125-138.

Williams, T., 1995, *Wexford Schools Hurling Survey*, Enniscorthy Press, Wexford.

Willis, P., 1981, "Cultural Production is Different from Cultural Reproduction is Different from Social Reproduction is Different from Reproduction", *Interchange*, Vol. 12, Nos. 2-3, pp. 48-67.

Woolger, C. and Power, T., 1993, "Parent and Sport Socialisation: Views from the Achievement Literature", *Journal of Sport Behaviour*, Vol. 16, No. 3, pp. 171-189.

Yang, X., Telamo, R. and Laasko, L., 1996, "Parents' Physical Activity, Socio-economic Status and Education as Predictors of Physical Activity and Sport among Children and Youths — A 12-Year Follow-Up Study", *International Review for Sociology of Sport*, Vol. 31, No. 3, pp. 273-289.

INDEX

CONTENTS

LIST OF TABLES AND FIGURES

ACKNOWLEDGEMENTS

I would like to acknowledge, with sincere gratitude, the following people: Dr Conor Galvin of University College Dublin for his invaluable advice and critical insight; Peter Smyth of the Irish Sports Council for organising financial support towards the publication costs; Waterford Institute of Technology for the initial seed funding to begin the research; the adolescents and sports leaders who took part in this research and who gave so generously of their time and opinions; the principals and staff, and in particular the PE staff, of the secondary schools in Waterford City; Milo O'Rathaile of WIT who gave so freely of his time and expertise in compiling the statistical data; David Givens and Brian Langan at The Liffey Press for their editing professionalism and for making this book a reality.

This book is dedicated to Patty, Darragh and Niamh

PREFACE

The research for this book was carried out between 1996 and 2000 in order to establish the general lifestyle patterns of Waterford adolescents and, in particular, the place of sport/physical activity within those lifestyles. In fact, it comprises the largest such study ever undertaken in this country, examining as it does the total population of school-going adolescents in a small city in the Republic of Ireland as well as from a number of other parts of Ireland. It was felt that highlighting the adolescent period is of particular importance as there is a growing realisation that the lifestyle patterns which are adopted in adolescence have critical implications for later life (Hendry et al., 1993; Mason, 1995).

There were two phases in the research. Phase One involved a questionnaire-based survey of the total population of school-going adolescents in Waterford City. A total of 3,315 adolescents were surveyed and this allowed the construction of a comprehensive picture of young people's sporting, leisure and lifestyle patterns in Waterford City. The second phase of the research was qualitative in nature and involved 312 interviewees, most of whom were a sub-set of the Phase One respondents. Others were added systematically to explore areas of discussion relating to particular and specific aspects of adolescent lifestyle not evident in the core survey base.

The findings from this research indicate that physical activity and sport do not dominate the life experiences of adolescents. While most adolescents claim to enjoy sport and physical activity, these may not be part of their lifestyle because of time spent on other activities, particularly the information and communication technologies. There were several areas identified which impacted significantly on the likelihood of the adolescent being involved in sport. Particular issues that were addressed include gender, social class groupings and other drivers and constraints to sports participation. The book concludes by identifying a number of trends that have been identified in relation to the sporting and physical activity patterns of adolescents in Ireland and by examining some of the policy issues that arise from the research.

Chapter 1

INTRODUCTION

The value of sport and physical activity to the normal healthy development of young people has a certain generally accepted standing. Pittman (1991) refers to the need for a holistic growth approach in adolescence which she terms "youth development" (p. 5). She describes this as the ongoing natural process of having one's basic needs met and the acquisition of life skills. Functioning well and feeling connected to a family entity and community are two critical elements in the process towards maturity and self-fulfilment. Sport can play a key role in such youth development. Of course, participation in sport is also promoted for other reasons. Many social functionalists have promoted sport and physical activity as a means of developing the physical, social and psychological skills of the individual. Similarly, sport has been touted as having a myriad of uses, including as an antidote to crime, a means of promoting culture, as an activity offering opportunities of breaking down social barriers, a means of preventing health problems and simply being an enjoyable thing to do.

As a result, the playing of sport and engaging in physical activity are being promoted by a variety of public, private and voluntary agencies. However, underlying the above beliefs are two fundamental assumptions in relation to young people and sport and physical activity which will be questioned. Firstly, there is the assumption that the vast majority of young people play sport and are physically active. Secondly, there is the widespread perception that all young people like sport and physical activity. These are questions of fundamental importance as the philosophy of sport and physical activity provision in Ireland would appear to be based on these premises. There appears to be ample provision for the adolescent who is interested in sport through school curricular and extracurricular provision as well as the variety of sporting clubs and bodies outside school. For the gifted sports person, there are possibilities of international competitions, sports grants, specialised coaching and even a professional sporting career. But the question has to be asked: what if the above premises are incorrect and that not alone are many adolescents not active but a significant number do not like any sport or physical activity? If this is the case, it may mean that there needs to be a fundamental rethink on how sport and physical activity is delivered by schools and sporting bodies. In fact, it is quite feasible that the needs of a significant number of Irish adolescents are being ignored and that sports providers are not even aware of this possibility.

There is arguably a view that Irish people are *sports mad*. In a preamble to the National Sports Strategy document in 1996,[1] the chairman John Treacy reflects this notion:

> Every weekend the playing fields of Ireland are packed with people pursuing their sporting passions. From the clash of hurleys in County Wexford, to the underage soccer matches in Tallaght, to the hundreds that walk our mountains and hills, to the women that run the pavement in preparation for the mini marathon, sport is an integral part of our existence and adds to the quality of life of all participants (1997, p. 5).

There may, however, be a wide divergence between the public perception about the levels of physical activity engaged in by the Irish population and the actual reality. However, there is little hard evidence to back up these views. In fact, there is a dearth of accurate and defensible information in relation to sports participation levels among adolescents in Ireland. This research aims to gather for the first time a detailed and com-

---

[1] This publication, entitled *Targeting Sporting Change in Ireland — Sport in Ireland 1997–2006 and Beyond,* is the first strategic plan drawn up by the Irish Government in relation to sport.

prehensive set of statistics which indicate the nature and extent of young people's involvement in sport in an Irish context.

LIFESTYLE AND ADOLESCENCE

This section aims to examine the concept of adolescent lifestyle and to offer a definitional context to the subject under discussion. There are many potential influences which may shape the lifestyles of Irish adolescents and the place of sport and physical activity within that lifestyle. The concept of *lifestyle* is a feature of modern society which is sometimes used to describe one's actions. The concept of lifestyles has been described as "patterns of action that differentiate people" (Chaney, 1996, p. 4). Distinctive patterns of social life are often summarised by the term *culture*. For example, Kephart defined culture in relation to lifestyle when he concluded that culture was "the total lifestyle of a people — their customs, attitudes and values, the shared understandings that bind them together as a society" (1982, p. 93). There has been an increased academic interest in the adolescent years as these years play a critical role in shaping the adult lifestyle which will be assumed by the individual. Adolescence is therefore a key stage in the possible sporting development of the young adult. It would appear critical for the development of sport and physical activity that the factors which encourage adolescents to be physically active are established. If adolescents become (or remain) physically active during this phase of their development, the likelihood is that they will remain active as they progress through adulthood.

Social scientists have long been intrigued by adolescents. They sometimes seem like a completely different species and their habits, idiosyncrasies and general behaviour have mystified grown-ups. While some academics and critics make positive assessments about the current status of adolescence, for the most part those interested in defining adolescence do so in the context of adolescence being a social problem (Epstein, 1998, p. 1). When Kurt Cobain, the lead singer with the rock group Nirvana, died from a self-inflicted shot gun blast, Gaines extrapolated on the influence of Cobain on adolescents in the following terms, which portray adolescents in a negative light:

his music was said to speak to a generation who are without
hope and have no illusions about a brighter future . . . these
are the children of suburbia, raised on McDonalds, shopping malls and MTV (1994, p. 60).

Davis (1990) has shown that, historically, the images held by
members of the general public in relation to adolescents in society have included the themes of rebellion, moodiness, angst,
delinquency, sinfulness, energy, excitement and idealistic
views of society. He further asserts that these images have been
retained in the adults' consciousness and reinforced by the
mass media and have created a stereotypical image of youth in
Britain in the 1990s. Another aspect of adolescent behaviour
which is often perceived as problematic, particularly by parents, is their egocentric nature. Elkind (1967) describes the
egocentric nature of adolescence which he tied in with the notion of "the imaginary audience". One example he gives is that
of the adolescent's appearance. Many teenagers are preoccu-
pied with the way they look to others and make the assumption
that others are equally involved (the imaginary audience). Thus
adolescents are continually constructing and reacting to their
imaginary audience, a fact which, according to Elkind, explains
a lot of adolescent behaviour, their self-consciousness, the wish
for privacy and the long hours spent in front of the mirror. Conger and Petersen (1984) have provided strong corroboration
for Elkind's views.

This book will move away from the idea that the lifestyles
and leisure activities of adolescents are by their nature problematic. Instead, it will attempt to examine adolescence in a
balanced manner and attempt to gain an understanding of what
it means to be young in a rapidly changing society in Ireland
today. The aim will be to examine what are the key influences
in the lives of adolescents. Problems will be identified but so
too will aspects of best practice, i.e. what kinds of approaches
appear to be particularly successful in relation to maximising
participation rates in physical activity and youth sport. Ultimately, the key area of interest is the promotion of sport/
physical activity amongst adolescents that will encourage lifelong participation. To put this into context, however, it is first of